T0381022

COMPASSIONATE ACTION

COMPASSIONATE ACTION

Chatral Rinpoche

Edited, Introduced,
and Annotated by
Zach Larson

Snow Lion
Boulder

Snow Lion
An imprint of Shambhala Publications, Inc.
2129 13th Street
Boulder, Colorado 80302
www.shambhala.com

Cover photograph by Carroll Schlenger; photo insert, thirteenth page, top, fourteenth page, top, Zach Larson; fifteenth page, top, sixteenth page, bottom, Raphaele Demandre; all other photo credits unknown.

Snow Lion is distributed worldwide by Penguin Random House, Inc., and its subsidiaries.

The Library of Congress Cataloguing-in-Publication Data
Saṇs-rgyas-rdo-rje, Bya-bral.
Compassionate action / Chatral Rinpoche; edited, introduced, and annotated by Zach Larson.
p. cm.
Includes bibliographical references and index.
ISBN 978-1-55939-271-6 (alk. paper)
1. Religious life—Buddhism. 2. Vegetarianism—Religious aspects—Buddhism. I. Larson, Zach, 1978– II. Title.
BQ7775.S25 2007
294.3'923092—dc22
[B]
2006039708

The authorized representative in the EU for product safety and compliance is eucomply OÜ, Pärnu mnt 139b-14, 11317 Tallinn, Estonia, hello@eucompliancepartner.com.

150698198

Dedicated to the long and healthy life
of the peerless Lord of Refuge
Chatral Sangye Dorje Rinpoche,
the profound lineages of teachings he represents,
and all those who follow his example in working
with great compassion to tirelessly bring all beings
to a state of perfect Enlightenment.

Contents

Foreword

I am happy to see that a few of His Holiness Chatral Rinpoche's teachings are being published under the title *Compassionate Action*. The incomparable sublime master Chatral Rinpoche is a true Buddha in person and his wisdom mind and compassionate activities are therefore limitless.

This book presents a glimpse of my kind root teacher's vision and activities and I am confident that the efforts of my student Zach Larson will be beneficial for true seekers in the West.

I pray that through the publication of these teaching all beings may realize the genuine teacher's wisdom mind and forever be truly compassionate and joyful.

Shyalpa Jigmed Tenzin Wangpo

Editor's Preface

I first met Chatral Rinpoche in 1999 while participating in the University of Wisconsin-Madison College Year in Nepal program. My two main identities at that time were as a vegetarian animal rights activist and as a practitioner in the Longchen Nyingthig tradition of the Nyingma School of Tibetan Buddhism. While in Nepal, I was a little discouraged to find so many Tibetan Buddhists unashamedly eating meat. Curious to find out how they justified eating meat with their Buddhist practice and how many Tibetans living in South Asia refrained from meat eating, I decided to engage in a six-month research project that spanned the length and breadth of India and Nepal, interviewing Tibetan refugees from all walks of life about the cultural convergence of Buddhism and meat eating.

As soon as I mentioned the idea of this project to my advisor, he mentioned Chatral Rinpoche, a revered lama who is well known for being a vegetarian and for his annual ceremony in Calcutta, where he releases tens of thousands of live fish originally caught to be eaten back into the ocean. In addition, I learned that he is considered to be one of the most highly realized practitioners in the very same Longchen Nyingthig lineage that I belong to! I went to see him in early October 1999 with my Tibetan language teacher and was blessed to arrive at a moment when he was giving a Guru Padmasambhava empowerment. My language teacher and I both gratefully received the empowerment and had a chance to speak with Rinpoche briefly. Being in his presence was an amazing experience. Much like being in the presence of His Holiness the Dalai Lama, one feels Chatral Rinpoche's powerful, compassionate energy radiating from his pure heart.

I traveled to the northern and southern extremes of India, interviewing Tibetan lamas, doctors, teachers, politicians, farmers, and businessmen living in refugee settlements. Of the dozens of people I interviewed, I met only three vegetarians. Upon my return to Nepal, my main objective was to interview Chatral Rinpoche about his views on Buddhism and meat eating. He graciously granted me an interview, which lasted about forty-five minutes (excerpts from that interview are included in Chapter 2). At the end of the interview, I mentioned the idea of translating some of his writings on Buddhism and meat eating into English. Rinpoche liked that idea and said that I could use the original texts he had used in composing his work for translation. I told him I would try to come back in a few years to complete the project, and four years later, I returned.

I discovered that Chatral Rinpoche had composed other excellent texts as well, such as "The Benefits of Saving the Lives of Other Beings" and "A Prayer to Avert Nuclear War." Therefore, this book was expanded into a compilation of Rinpoche's teachings and an account of his life story. The selections of Rinpoche's writings included herein have been translated by myself, unless otherwise noted. The translation of Rinpoche's essay "On Meat Eating" by Geshe Thupten Phelgye and Aaron Gross has been revised. Adam Pearcey's translation of Rinpoche's "Words of Advice" also includes some minor revisions.

This is the first book in English by this wonderful man, though probably not the last. By his great example, may all beings reach the highest state of perfect Enlightenment!

— Zach Larson

Acknowledgments

First and foremost, immeasurable gratitude to Chatral Rinpoche for his boundless compassion in helping the beings of this degenerate age. Tsetan Chonjore and Thinley Dhondrup offered kind support in the translation of Advice for Nyingma Practitioners. Many thanks to Matthieu Ricard for his warm support and to Jeanne Larson for her proofreading expertise. My sincere appreciation to Shyalpa Rinpoche, his boundless wisdom, and the sangha of Rangrig Yeshe, for being my refuge. Thanks to Adam Pearcey and Eric Pema Kunsang for their inspiring kindness. This work was completed near the cave of Guru Padmasambhava in Yangleshöd, Nepal, and I am ever grateful for his endless blessings.

Introduction

The nature of reality according to the Vajrayana School of Tibetan Buddhism can be described as emptiness with compassion as its very essence. The symbol of the *vajra* — from which the school gets its name — is representative of compassionate action. This symbol serves as the pinnacle for the crown Chatral Rinpoche is wearing in the cover photograph and likewise great compassion is the core energy behind his every action.

Chatral Rinpoche embodies the bodhisattva vow — the vow to help all beings in this and all future lives to reach enlightenment — for he tirelessly engages in compassionate activities to impartially help both humans and animals. Not only does he refrain from harming beings — by maintaining a strict vegetarian diet — he also saves the lives of countless beings each year, giving them a chance to die in peace and attain a higher rebirth and a better chance to achieve enlightenment in the next life.

The Nyingma lineage teachings that Chatral Rinpoche flawlessly preserves have a long-standing tradition of compassion that transcends normal human limitations. However, few have lived as uncompromisingly in their dedication to the bodhisattva ideal as Chatral Rinpoche. Patrul Rinpoche (1808–87), the great master who was the teacher of Chatral Rinpoche's root guru's teacher, comes to mind as someone who had similar qualities. The story is told that Patrul Rinpoche was traveling with a poor widow to a town in the Kham region of eastern Tibet, helping her cook and take care of her children, even carrying her children on his back as they walked along. When they arrived at the town, Patrul Rinpoche excused himself, saying he had some business to take care of. The widow had heard of a great lama giving a talk at the local monastery that night and was shocked to see her traveling companion on a throne instructing the vast assembly! He asked that all of the offerings made at the end of the teaching be given to that poor widow.

Buddha Shakyamuni is well known for his infinitely vast compassion. In a story of one of his past lives, he gave up his body as sustenance for a starving tiger that had several cubs to feed. As Prince Siddhartha, he saved the life of a swan that his brother had shot with an arrow, removing the arrow and nurturing the swan back to health. Chatral Rinpoche's full name is Chatral Sangye Dorje Rinpoche. "Sangye" is the Tibetan word for Buddha and "Dorje" means *vajra* (an indestructible diamond scepter). There is no doubt that Chatral Rinpoche's compassion is equal to that of Buddha Shakyamuni himself.

One cannot attain enlightenment only by understanding the Buddha's teachings in one's mind; great compassion is essential. There is a story of Asanga — the founder of the Yogachara School of Mahayana

Buddhism — that shows the importance of compassion in being able to attain realization. Asanga engaged in the practice of Buddha Maitreya for twelve years, hoping to have a sign or vision of him. After no such vision came, he became discouraged and began to head back to his hometown. Along the way, he saw an emaciated and crippled dog that was crawling with maggots. Asanga was overcome with compassion and cut off a piece of his own flesh to feed the dog. He wanted to remove the maggots from the dog, but did not want to harm them, so decided to use his tongue to remove them. As he closed his eyes and stuck out his tongue, suddenly the Buddha Maitreya appeared to him in place of the dog. Buddha Maitreya gave Asanga the teachings he had been waiting for, because through this act of great compassion he proved he was finally ready to receive them.

The "four immeasurables" — boundless loving-kindness, boundless compassion for all beings, boundless joy (in the happiness of others), and boundless equanimity (desire to help all beings regardless of size or status) — are the foundations of Mahayana Buddhism and the bodhisattva path. In the essays and prayers contained in this book, Chatral Rinpoche discusses all four "immeasurables." In "The Benefits of Saving the Lives of Other Beings," he describes the path of loving kindness. In "On Meat Eating," he urges Buddhists to look on animals with compassion and refrain from eating meat. In "Thangtong Gyalpo's Aspiration Prayer for the Liberation of Fish," he gives us a practice for cultivating joy in being able to help the helpless. In "Advice for Nyingma Practitioners," he describes equanimity in its different aspects: looking at all beings as having been one's parents in past lifetimes and reminding us that anyone can be a holder of the Buddha's teachings if they live according to the Dharma, not just monks and lamas of high status.

Chatral Rinpoche is now in his 90s, yet continues to engage in acts of compassion without growing weary. Through his wonderful teachings and the example of his amazing life as recounted in this book, may all be inspired to enhance the compassion of their own spiritual practice. May all who have taken the bodhisattva vow, or plan to take it in the future, follow Chatral Rinpoche's same great standard of helping all beings with an uncompromising and unshakable loving-kindness. In this way, the prayer "May all beings attain unsurpassed perfect Enlightenment" can one day become a reality.

1   Chatral Rinpoche
The Life of a Legend

Kyabje[1] Chatral Sangye Dorje Rinpoche is one of the most accomplished Tibetan Buddhist yogis alive today. In 1947 he had the lofty status of being the head spiritual master of the political leader of Tibet, Regent Reting, but he has always preferred to live as a humble yogi in a simple dwelling without the distractions of fame and fortune. He practices what he preaches without compromise and as a result is beloved throughout the Himalayan region by people of all faiths.

Rinpoche was born in 1913 in the Nyak Adzi Valley in Kham, Tibet to pious members of the Abse tribal group named Pema Döndrub (father) and Sönam Tso (mother).[2] The day after his birth, a local lama named Asey Bigo Tulku Nyima Gyaltsen came to Pema and Sonam's house to tell them of a vision he had the day before about Rinpoche's emergence, in which a white donkey loaded down with Buddhist scriptures came to Pema and Sonam's house and delivered the texts to them. In accordance with this vision, he bestowed upon the newborn the name Trogyal Dorje, which means "Adamantine Wrathful Victorious One."

Chatral Rinpoche's family moved to Amdo with their tribal group when he was a small child. At age fifteen, Rinpoche decided to leave his family in order to study and practice Buddhism with the masters of the area. This act of renunciation began his life-long journey as a carefree yogi seeking enlightenment at any cost in order to effectively help other beings with compassion. From the onset, Rinpoche was highly principled, traveling exclusively on foot and refusing a horse when offered. He stayed only in hermitages, caves, or his small tent in order to avoid involvement with householders and their worldly preoccupations.

The following text by the Nyingma master Kyabje Dudjom Rinpoche, excerpted from his *Practice of the Mountain Retreat Expounded Simply and Directly in Its Essential Nakedness*, seems to be the yogi code of ethics that Chatral Rinpoche has lived by since he left home:

> It is said: "By abandoning one's Fatherland half of the Dharma is accomplished." So, leaving your Fatherland behind, wander through unknown countries. Parting from your friends and relatives in a pleasant way, ignore those who try to dissuade you from practicing the Dharma. Giving away your possessions, rely on whatever alms come your way. Understanding all desirable things to be the obstacles linked with bad habits, develop a disinterested mind. If — of possessions and so on — you don't know how to be content with just a little, once

you've got one you'll want two and it won't be difficult for the deceiving demon of desirable objects to enter your life…

You should take along the Path all connections, both with people who hold you in good esteem and treat you well and with people who dislike you and treat you badly; good or bad, without caring at all, accept them with pure and good wishes. At all times inwardly keep your spirits high without losing courage and outwardly, on the path of action, remain humble. Wear worn-out clothes. Consider everyone — good, bad or neutral — above yourself. Live frugally and remain steadily in mountain hermitages. Fix your ambition on the condition of a beggar…

Even when meditation has penetrated your mind, you need to cultivate it continuously; otherwise the deep instructions will be left on the pages of the books and your mind, your Dharma and your practice will become impervious so that the emergence of genuine meditation will never come. You old meditators, still novices in practice, watch out — there's a danger that you may die with your head encrusted with salt.[3]

Chatral Rinpoche received transmissions of the *terma*[4] cycle of Terton Dudjom Lingpa (1835–1903) from the Terton's son Dorje Dradül (1891–1959). Rinpoche would later become the Vajra Regent or Chief Lineage Holder of this cycle of teachings, known as Dudjom Tersar.[5] Another one of Rinpoche's main early teachers was Khandro Dewai Dorje (1899–1952), who was a daughter-in-law of

Terton Dudjom Lingpa. She passed on to Rinpoche the terma cycle teachings of Sera Khandro and he became the principal lineage holder of this tradition as well.[6]

At this time, Chatral Rinpoche met his root guru, Khenpo Ngawang Palzang (1879–1941) of Kathok Monastery.[7] The great Khenpo had been the heart disciple of Patrul Rinpoche's main student, Lungtok Tenpai Nyima (1829–1901),[8] and was considered to be a manifestation of the ninth century Dzogchen[9] master Vimalamitra. Khenpo Ngakchung gave Chatral Rinpoche many teachings and transmissions — particularly of the Longchen Nyingthig tradition[10] — and for the next six years Rinpoche studied under him, completing his *ngöndro*[11] and practicing *trekchöd*[12] and *tögyal,*[13] which are some of the most advanced practices of Dzogchen. Rinpoche studied with other masters at Kathok Monastery as well, in addition to the great Khyentse Chökyi Lodrö (1893–1959)[14] from Dzongsar Monastery, which (like Kathok) is in the Derge region of Kham.

Khenpo Ngawang Palzang knew Rinpoche was very special and acknowledged him to be his closest disciple, explaining that, "his mind and my mind are no different."[15] He bestowed upon Rinpoche the name Chatral Sangye Dorje, which means "Indestructible Buddha who has Abandoned all Mundane Activities."

The first time Chatral Rinpoche's greatness became revealed to others was at a large worship service at Kathok Monastery, attended by several high lamas sitting on lofty thrones. Rinpoche sat in the back on a simple meditation cushion with a few hundred other monks. During the service, Khenpo Ngawang Palzang remarked:

Among all of you here today, there are less than ten people who have one-tenth of my realization. Then, there are less than five of you who have half of my realization. Finally, there is only one person here whose realization is no different from mine, and he is Chatral Sangye Dorje. He can now represent me to transmit the teachings and his merits are the same as mine.[16]

This proclamation caused quite a stir in the assembly hall and afterward people came to congratulate Rinpoche. Preparations began for a grand ceremony to honor Rinpoche in his new status. Rinpoche was not one for all this attention and praise and so snuck away in the middle of the night with his tent to continue his practice alone in the wilderness. The next day when they came to honor him, they found his room empty with no indictaion of where he went. Once again, he lived up to his name Chatral, which can be translated as "hermit."

Chatral Rinpoche once explained, "We abide nowhere, we possess nothing."[17] In the ultimate sense, this is a profound statement on the impermanence of life and emptiness of all things. In the conventional sense, this is how a yogi like Chatral Rinpoche actually lived in Tibet. Having no household or possessions to weigh on one's mind, one is completely free to practice the Dharma. As far as the seeming adversity of physical discomforts and irregular meals, Dudjom Rinpoche explained, "When realization becomes as vast as space, all adverse conditions arise as friends."[18]

In 1947 the regent-king of Tibet, Reting, who was the political leader of the country until the current Dalai Lama came of age, requested teachings from Khenpo Ngakchung, who told him, "I am too old now for transmitting teachings to you. I have a disciple whose mind and realization is the same as mine and he is called Chatral Sangye Dorje. You can go ask him for teachings."[19]

Regent Reting looked all over for Chatral Rinpoche and found him meditating in a remote mountain cave. Upon hearing his request, Rinpoche replied, "I am sorry, there is nothing special about me and I have nothing to teach you. Please go elsewhere for teachings!"[20] The Regent then produced a letter by Khenpo Ngakchung to support his request, and so Rinpoche reluctantly agreed to go to Lhasa to teach Regent Reting.

People from all over poured into Lhasa to meet Rinpoche and recieve teachings and blessings from him. This included high-ranking lamas, political leaders, and common laypeople, who made many offerings to Rinpoche. Naturally, he saw all of this attention as a distraction for his spiritual development. He requested to have some time to meditate in a remote area away from Lhasa. The Regent agreed and sent a large entourage of servants and guards to escort Rinpoche on his journey. After they arrived, Rinpoche asked the group of men to return to Lhasa so that he could meditate in solitude. The Regent did not want his teacher to be alone, so sent some guards back to locate Rinpoche. Along the way, they found a poor beggar dressed in royal brocade robes. Chatral Rinpoche had traded his fancy outfit for beggar's rags in true yogi style!

Another great spiritual master who came into Chatral Rinpoche's life was Kyabje Dudjom Rinpoche, Jigdral Yeshe Dorje, who was an incarnation of Terton Dudjom Lingpa.[21] Dudjom Rinpoche transmitted to Chatral Rinpoche the complete cycle of the Dudjom Tersar teachings, naming him the Vajra Regent of the tradition. He wrote the following about Chatral Rinpoche:

> To all endowed with sentience — beings large and small — who live and circle within the realms of existence; at this time the Awareness-Holder Trogyal Dorje [Chatral Rinpoche] has received from me the oral lineage instructions of the profound teaching — heart-blood of the dakinis.[22] I have entrusted him with the lineage of the meaning, empowered him as the person to act as my Regent to guide beings, and encouraged him to impartially steer the ship of disciples to the path of freedom.
>
> Therefore, any gods, demons or humans who help Trogyal Dorje in an appropriate manner will naturally gain benefit and happiness in this and future lifetimes. However, if even the slightest thoughts or acts of wrongful animosity toward him should arise, the armies of imperious guardians of the doctrine — endowed with wrathful power and eyes of wisdom — will come to his assistance. They will most certainly sever the life force of beings that have form or block the senses of those without form and banish their name that remains. Where there is a chance of such profit or loss, be extremely careful![23]

Chatral Rinpoche became Dudjom Rinpoche's heart disciple and took his responsibility as Dudjom Tersar Regent very seriously, protecting his precious teacher and lineage from corrupting influences.

One day in the early 1950s, Dudjom Rinpoche was receiving an empowerment of a terma from the Chokgyur Lingpa tradition from Tulku Urgyen Rinpoche when Chatral Rinpoche came by. Tulku Urgyen Rinpoche was a relative unknown at that time and Chatral Rinpoche was suspicious as to his qualifications for giving an empowerment to his beloved master. Tulku Urgyen Rinpoche describes his exchange with Chatral Rinpoche:

> Our conversation began like this: "You, lama! Where are you from?" he demanded brusquely.
> "I am from Nangchen."
> "From where in Nangchen?"
> "I am a descendant of Chokgyur Lingpa."
> "I've been to Tsikey and I didn't see you there."
> "I didn't always stay at Tsikey."
> "Then where are you from? Out with it!"
> "Chokgyur Lingpa's daughter, Könchok Paldrön, had four sons, one of whom was my father."
> "Hmmm…hmmm…I had heard that you were supposed to be the nephew of Neten Chokling. I know him from Dzongsar, where he came to visit Dzongsar Khyentse, but I've never heard that he had a lama nephew. Now I hear that *our* Dudjom Rinoche is receiving the *Three Sections*[24] from such a nephew, and we all know that plenty of these so-called Khampa lamas come here to Central Tibet to try out their various tricks. So, I was wondering if you were just another one of them. Hmmm…"

He was staring at me with his big eyes glaring the whole time. "A lot of Khampa lamas come here and cheat people by giving empowerments to which they have no lineage."

Dudjom Rinpoche, who was sitting right there, broke in and said, "It was I who asked him to give this transmission."

And soon [Dudjom and Chatral Rinpoche] began to crack one joke after another, during which Chatral Rinpoche turned to me with a smirk and said, "Okay, I guess you are not a fake after all — you can go ahead and give him the empowerment then."[25]

Chatral Rinpoche spent a great deal of his time practicing in caves blessed by Guru Padmasambhava,[26] the founder of Tibetan Buddhism and source of the terma teachings that are the basis for many of the lineages of the Nyingma School.[27] Chatral Rinpoche is actually considered to be the mind manifestation of Guru Padmasambhava's, based on prophecies about Rinpoche's emergence and his proven wisdom.[28]

In the late 1950s, Chatral Rinpoche moved to Bhutan. He was not forced out by the events of March 10, 1959 like many other Tibetans,[29] but went to Bhutan of his own free will. This may be indicative of his being the manifestation of Guru Padmasambhava's mind, as Guru Rinpoche had predicted that the Tibetan people would be displaced from their homeland at the advent of the modern age and Chatral Rinpoche seemed to know that the time was right for him to travel to other areas in the Himalayas.[30] When he was asked what this trip was like for him, he smiled and replied, "Completely free, light, and happy."[31]

Chatral Rinpoche traveled to the neighboring Himalayan region of Darjeeling, where he restored a simple temple and turned it into a three-year meditation retreat center for Longchen Nyingthig practice. This was the first such center built by a Tibetan outside of Tibet. Rinpoche then went to some of the major Buddhist pilgrimage sites in India. While visiting the site of the Buddha's enlightenment in 1960, he made a firm commitment that would become a famous part of his identity. He said, "I went to Bodhgaya and made a vow to all the buddhas and bodhisattvas to give up meat and alcohol."[32] Rinpoche is quite unique in his intensely disciplined stance on this issue and this is part of what makes him so revered by those who know him.

A few years later, he met Kusho Kamala, daughter of Terton Tulzhok Lingpa, who became his *sangyüm*.[33] They have two daughters, Saraswati and Tara Devi. Saraswati serves as his main assistant and speaks fluent English. She is considered to be an emanation of the dakini Sera Khandro.

In 1968 in Darjeeling, Chatral Rinpoche had a famous meeting with the Trappist monk Father Thomas Merton, an advanced Zen Buddhist practitioner held in high regard by other Buddhists. Merton wrote of the encounter,

> …and there was Chatral, the greatest Rinpoche that I have met so far and a very impressive person. Chatral looked like a vigorous old peasant in a Bhutanese jacket tied at the neck with thongs and a red woolen cap on his head. He had a week's growth of beard, bright eyes, a strong voice and was

very articulate. We started talking about Dzogchen and Nyingma meditation and "direct realization" and soon saw that we agreed very well. We must have talked for two hours or more, covering all sorts of ground, mostly around the idea of Dzogchen but also taking in some points of Christian doctrine compared with Buddhist Dharmakaya,[34] the Risen Christ, suffering, compassion for all creatures, motives for "helping others," but all leading back to Dzogchen, the ultimate emptiness, the unity of *shunyata* [emptiness] and *karuna* [compassion], going "beyond the Dharmakaya" and "beyond God" to the ultimate perfect emptiness.

He said he had meditated in solitude for thirty years or more and had not attained perfect emptiness and I said I hadn't either. The unspoken or half-spoken message of the talk was our complete understanding of each other as people who were somehow on the edge of great realization and knew it and were trying, somehow or other, to go out and get lost in it — and that it was a grace for us to meet one another. I wish I could see more of Chatral. He burst out and called me a Rangjung Sangay (which apparently means a "natural Buddha") and said that he had been named a Sangay Dorje. He wrote "Rangjung Sangay" for me in Tibetan and said that when I entered the "great kingdom" and "the palace," then America and all that was in it would seem like nothing. He told me, seriously, that perhaps he and I would attain complete Buddhahood in our next lives, perhaps even in this life, and the parting note was a kind of compact that we would both do our best to make

11

it in this life. I was profoundly moved, because he is so obviously a great man, the true practitioner of Dzogchen, the best of the Nyingmapa lamas, marked by complete simplicity and freedom…If I were going to settle down with a Tibetan guru, I think Chatral would be the one I'd choose.[35]

Merton was later overheard saying "That is the greatest man I ever met. He is my teacher."

Chatral Rinpoche was relentless in his study and practice. In India, he received teachings from Kalu Rinpoche, who became his close friend, and the Sixteenth Karmapa Rangjung Rigpe Dorje. He received teachings from over one hundred masters in all, from many traditions of Tibetan Buddhism. The breadth of his scholarship is evident in his writing, as he quotes texts from a myriad of traditions to support the points he makes in his essays.

Chatral Rinpoche has founded or restored meditation retreat centers in Bhutan, India, and Nepal as well as overseen the construction of several stupas.[36] Dudjom Rinpoche consecrated Rinpoche's center in Darjeeling in 1962 and around ten years later helped Rinpoche start a center in Yangleshöd, Nepal, which he thought would be a very auspicious place, as Guru Padmasambhava had accomplished some important practices there. This monastery, which lies on the outer rim of the Kathmandu Valley and is known as Rigzin Drubpe Ghatsal, "Joyous Grove in the Place of the Accomplishment of the Glorious Awareness-Holder," was one of Rinpoche's primary residences for many years. Compared to many other lamas who have lavish, spacious quarters, Rinpoche's residence here is incredibly humble and cozy.

Many thousands of people in the Himalayan region consider Chatral Rinpoche to be their root guru because, through his compassionate action and profound wisdom, he is a perfect embodiment of the Buddha's teachings. However, he is very selective about those he actually gives teachings to. He is fully aware that most of the people who ask him for teachings are not a fraction as serious about their practice as he is, so doesn't bother to waste the precious nectar of his teachings on an unsuitable vessel. Rinpoche explains, "There are three kinds of Dharma practitioners: firstly, there are those who look like practitioners outwardly, but inwardly they are not real practitioners; secondly, there are those who talk very high, but have no realization at all; thirdly there are those who do not look like practitioners outwardly, but who are in fact genuine practitioners inside."[37] Rinpoche therefore will not transmit any higher-level teachings to those who have studied with him for less than six years — sufficient time for them to prove themselves as genuine practitioners.

Westerners especially are treated with suspicion. Too many come to see Rinpoche wanting the ultimate teachings of Dzogchen without being remotely qualified to receive or understand them. There is a story of a wealthy person from the United States who set big stacks of American dollar bills in front of Rinpoche, saying that if Rinpoche gave him Dzogchen teachings, then he would give him all of this money. Rinpoche told him briskly to take his money away and declined to give him teachings. The sacred teachings certainly cannot be bought with bribes; one must earn the right to receive them.[38]

In the Longchen Nyingthig tradition, it is not uncommon for higher-level teachings to be passed on to only one or two of a master's most dedicated and gifted disciples. Khenpo Ngawang Palzang's root guru Nyoshul Lungtok transmitted some of the Longchen Nyingthig teachings and empowerments to the great Khenpo exclusively. These types of teachings are regarded as secret and are preserved by a direct one-to-one transmission from a realized master to a fully qualified disciple.

One such person who was ready to receive Chatral Rinpoche's profound teachings was a remarkable practitioner known as Yüm Kusho-la, the consort of Tulku Urgyen Rinpoche. The following is an account of this transmission of teachings, which took place in the final days of her life, written by her son Chökyi Nyima Rinpoche:[39]

Chatral Rinpoche...came to see her. She had much devotion to him. She asked him for a Vajrasattva wong [empowerment] and requested that he teach her "The Four Parts Without Three."[40] This is the ultimate view of trekchöd. He taught for a long time. Unfortunately, we did not tape record the teaching, but he might not have wanted it to be taped anyway. Nevertheless, the teaching was very long and clear. Finally Chatral Rinpoche said, "Okay, let's mingle our minds. Rest in equanimity." We all knew — especially her doctors — that my mother was very weak, but at that moment she said "AH" very strongly. Her eyes were completely wide open. There was no indication of any pain; instead, she appeared very relaxed. I looked at my watch. She remained in that state for a full five minutes. I was suddenly worried that she might be dying. I thought, "What's wrong?" I looked at Chatral Rinpoche and he was just sitting there in meditation. That made me relax and I understood that we should then all just remain in rigpa.⁴¹

After five minutes, she "returned back." She had been remaining in the view of the "four parts without three" without speaking. Afterwards, she started to communicate and she thanked Chatral Rinpoche. He said, "I'm very happy you understood this teaching. I knew you were a good practitioner, but I didn't realize you had this high level of awareness. Today I see that, so I respect you, and I'm proud to know you. You are a good example for everyone."

Later Chatral Rinpoche joined my father and me for lunch in another room. For more than one hour, we ate and talked. My father didn't ask much, but I asked Chatral Rinpoche, "What happened? What did my mother experience?" He looked at me very seriously and said, "Well. It was a very wonderful thing. She mingled space and awareness. Only the foremost practitioner is able to do that, especially in the face of such strong pain and severe illness. Only today did I realize that Yüm Kusho-la is such an advanced practitioner. This is a good example for us all. Now watch. There will be other amazing signs. It would be good if everyone with a link to Yüm Kusho-la can meet her, offer a white scarf, make prostration, and request to mingle their mind with hers."⁴²

Chatral Rinpoche does not spend a lot of his time giving teachings, as only a very few people are qualified to receive teachings like this. Instead, he tirelessly engages in virtuous activity, culminating in his famous annual trip to Calcutta, where he frees seventy truck-loads of live fish back into a part of the Indian Ocean where fishing is prohibited, praying for each and every one. He receives donations from around the world for this great act of compassion, which is the subject of one of his essays in this book. Still, he is very supportive of serious practitioners, traveling to his different retreat centers as often as he can to check on their progress. He also graciously offers guidance to those from other faiths who meet with him. Recently, when an Anglican priest asked him for a teaching, Rinpoche said, "Just decide what is the most important thing Jesus ever said, and then take it as far as you can." This turned out to be the most profound advice the priest had ever received and it served to deepen his understanding and faith.

Chatral Rinpoche makes appearances to support his disciples through dreams and visions. In 1997, at the beginning of a weekend retreat in San Francisco, Lama Tharchin Rinpoche told his students that Chatral Rinpoche had appeared to him in a dream, asking that Lama Tharchin and his students accumulate one hundred million recitations of Guru Padmasambhava's seven-line prayer[43] in order to remove obstacles to Lama Tharchin's health, benefit all beings, and help bring peace to the world during this degenerate age.[44]

Following the Tibetan New Year in 2000, hundreds of pious Buddhists gathered at Rinpoche's center in Yangleshöd from different parts of the Himalayan region, requesting Rinpoche's blessings for the new millennium. They camped out in tents near his monastery and waited patiently for days. At the most auspicious time, Rinpoche gave them all a long-life initiation. After the initiation, the group sang beautiful songs praising the great activities and glory of their exalted master and danced joyfully.

Rinpoche's vast knowledge is by no means limited to Buddhist philosophy. He is also an expert on thangka painting, ritual music and dance and many other subjects. Thangka painter Lama Tsondru Sangpo writes:

> Most important [for me] has been the continuous personal guidance I have received from Chatral Sangye Dorje Rinpoche, my spiritual protector for this and all future lives. He blesses me again and again with tremendously important yet scarcely known advice on the crucial points of thangka painting and gives me extensive, detailed instruction on the specific design and posture of each particular deity.[45]

Chatral Rinpoche is renowned for being incorruptible and insistent on doing things the right way. In the Tibetan Buddhist tradition, when someone dies, it is standard to leave them for three days to allow ample time for the consciousness to leave the body and hopefully enter into a Pureland realm or at least a high rebirth. According to Sogyal Rinpoche, "[Chatral Rinpoche] told people who were complaining that a corpse might smell if it was kept in hot weather [for three days]; 'It's not as though you have to eat it, or try to sell it.' "[46]

In 2002, an unfortunate incident occurred at one of Rinpoche's centers in the Darjeeling area. An American man who had been in

India studying Tibetan Buddhism paid a visit to Rinpoche. During a prayer service, the man asked Rinpoche for a private meeting to discuss "something important." When Rinpoche declined, the man leaped up and began to choke him. The man was subdued by Rinpoche's attendants and disciples and asked to leave. The man continued to act out, and when they managed to bring him outside of the main gates of the center, he had a tantrum and was verbally abusive. The police came and took him away, but the incident was very traumatizing to everyone involved and, as a result, it is now more difficult for Westerners who have not previously met Rinpoche to have an audience with him. The attacker spent some time in a mental health facility before being deported from India for attacking another person in South India later that year. Illustrative of what a remarkable bodhisattva Rinpoche is, he and his wife, Sangyüm Kusho Kamala, called the man when he returned to the United States out of concern for his well-being.

Even under the most trying of circumstances, Rinpoche's great compassion proves to be unflappable. The famous work *The Thirty-seven Practices of a Bodhisattva* by Ngulchu Gyalsas Thogmed Zangpo (fourteenth century) lists the thirteenth practice of a bodhisattva as follows:

Although we are not guilty of any offense and have never harmed anyone in our life, if someone deluded should threaten to kill us because he is crazed with a tormented mind, then mercifully wishing for him not to suffer further misfortune because of his state, selflessly taking on the effects of his action, is the practice of a bodhisattva.[47]

Chatral Rinpoche has been asked by many of his students to write an autobiographical account of his life. To accommodate their request, he wrote the following poetic lines.

A Reply in Three Syllables

An autobiographical account containing direct teachings that hit the vital point, written about a present-day misleading trickster like myself, is this.

May the spiritual master and the Three Jewels think of me!

I am an old man, at the end of my eighty-seventh year and approaching my eighty-eighth. Many persons close to or distant from me have asked, "Please write an autobiographical account of your life to help your followers." I have recognized this as an obstacle and a hindrance to liberation and I see no need to write many misleading words. As no one is better informed than me on this subject, I will act as my own witness and reply with this composition, *A Reply in Three Syllables:*[48]

The three qualities of ethics, Samadhi,[49] and insight,
Untainted and proven through direct perception,
Like dry moss, free from the dampness of pretentious
     falsehood,
I consumed in the space of blazing fire
With the radiant syllable RAM.

A religious facade, the jumble of materialism and
    Dharma,
I surely knew was not the friend of effective practice.
So I tossed the dry ashes of deceit and insensitivity
To the wind from the mountaintop, as the syllable YAM.

Funds given for the living and the dead, a hindrance to
    freedom,
And the schemes to collect, hoard, and invest them to
    build sacred objects,
I resolved to cleanse away with the clear stream of
    renunciation, detachment, and revulsion,
With the elemental syllable KHAM.[50]

Chatral Rinpoche's legend will undoubtedly live on for many generations. In 2003, he was honored as one of the most influential figures in Nepal during a ceremony in Kathmandu. As Rinpoche is already fully realized, he did not worry about the attention and praise of this event affecting his practice this time and attended the ceremony along with many of his students and friends. Showing that he is still a carefree yogi at heart, he wore a traditional Nepali topi hat during the ceremony — likely a first for a Tibetan Buddhist master!

Despite the adulation of countless thousands in the Himalayan region, Rinpoche remains as humble as ever. He once said,

I am just an ordinary sentient being and there is nothing special about me. I just follow the teachings of Lord Buddha. Without any cheating on my part, I stand firmly on the ground in practicing the Dharma and in helping all sentient beings. I wish that all sentient beings could let go of the acts of self-deception and self-aggrandizement, so that they can really practice the Dharma in order to liberate themselves from cyclic existence and to help other sentient beings. Otherwise, it will be too late when they are feeling remorseful![51]

2 Chatral Rinpoche's Steadfast Commitment to Ethics

Chatral Rinpoche is renowned in the Tibetan community for his peerless spiritual discipline, especially when it comes to refraining from eating meat. Meat eating is an entrenched aspect of Tibetan culture, and there are very few who can do without it for long. His Holiness the Dalai Lama became a vegetarian in 1966, but when he fell ill with Hepatitis B his doctors insisted he start to eat meat again, which he continues to do today in moderate quantities. A few contemporary masters — such as Kangyur Rinpoche — were also known for being strict vegetarians, but they tend to be the exception.

As a student in the University of Wisconsin-Madison College Year in Nepal Program in 2000, I was studying how Tibetans view the cultural convergence of Buddhism and meat eating. Some excerpts from my interview with Chatral Rinpoche follow.[52]

Compassionate Action

An Interview with Chatral Rinpoche

Question: Why did you decide to stop eating meat? How old were you when you made this decision?
Rinpoche: It is written in many Theravadayana and Mahayana texts that one should not eat meat. There is also a Vajrayana text that says the same thing, that one should not enjoy meat or alcohol. Because of this I am following the instructions of Shakyamuni Buddha. Being a religious person, I don't take meat or alcohol and at the same time I try to tell other people not to consume these things. This is my reason — I'm just trying to motivate other people. I was forty-seven years old when I went to Bodhgaya and made a vow to all of the buddhas and bodhisattvas to give up meat and alcohol.

Question: Why do you think vegetarianism is an important aspect of practicing the Dharma?
Rinpoche: If you take meat, it goes against the vows one takes in seeking refuge in the Buddha, Dharma, and Sangha. Because when you take meat you have to take a being's life. So I gave it up.

Question: Some claim that one can help the animals one eats by praying for them, and thus eating meat is compassionate. Other than for the most accomplished yogis and lamas, what do you make of this claim?
Rinpoche: With supernatural powers gained through certain meditation practices, it is true that there are some realized beings who can revive animals from the dead and help them reach a higher rebirth

24

or enlightenment by consuming small amounts of their flesh. But this is not done for sustenance, only for the purpose of helping that animal. I personally do not have that power and, because of that, I never eat meat. Eating meat in one's diet is much different than eating flesh to liberate a being through supernatural powers. I am just an ordinary practitioner who really doesn't have these qualities. So, if I ate meat it would be the same if you or any other lay person ate meat. I would be committing a sin and I would be getting negative karma. I don't pretend as if I have special powers and eat meat, I just avoid it altogether.

Question: Do you know other lamas who are vegetarian?
Rinpoche: I know many of them from Tibet. There are Nyingmapa, Sakyapa, and Gelukpa vegetarians in Tibet. Compared to the many meat-eating lamas, vegetarian lamas are very few, though. I'm eighty-eight and during my experience I have come across many lamas in Kham, Amdo — all parts of Tibet — who don't eat meat. There are lamas who eat meat and those who don't. At my monastery in Tibet there are also lamas who take meat and those who don't.

Question: Many Buddhist practitioners in the United States eat meat because their Tibetan lamas eat meat. What do you make of this?
Rinpoche: Many great siddhas in India drank enormous amounts of alcohol and developed magical powers. One of these mahasiddhas, Virupa, kept drinking alcohol all day and suspended the sun in the sky and kept it from setting.[53] Naropa, Tilopa — these were great masters. If you can acquire supernatural powers, you don't need to

follow the same standards of normal people and you can drink alcohol and eat meat. Those who have supernatural powers can still give great teachings and benefit all sentient beings. It all depends on the level of realization one has achieved. A lama who enjoys meat and alcohol can still bring people on the right path, so long as they have developed supernatural powers.

Question: Do you see Tibetan Buddhists in exile making a sincere effort to reduce their meat consumption and become vegetarian, or has meat eating become an entrenched aspect of Tibetan culture?

Rinpoche: In Tibet, there's only meat and *tsampa* [roasted barley flour] — there is no other staple food. Tibet is at a high altitude and the climate is tundralike. There are not many fruits and vegetables. After coming to South Asia, you really don't have to follow the Tibetan custom of meat and *tsampa*. There are many types of fruits and vegetables, nutritional supplements — all kinds of good foods. Everything is available. So there is really no need to talk about the customs of Tibet as an excuse for eating meat. From my experience, not eating meat has many benefits. I'm eighty-eight and ever since I stopped eating meat, I haven't had any major sickness. When I sleep, I sleep well. When I get up, I can walk right away. When I read religious texts, I can see them properly. I have very good hearing and can listen attentively. These are the qualities I have experienced from not eating meat. I didn't get sick or die when I stopped eating meat; no negative consequences came to me. I can travel by vehicle, airplane, or train without getting nauseous or dizzy and I never get headaches. I am a human being formed with flesh and blood like anyone else and am proof that giving up meat does not make one ill like many Tibetans seem to think. I'm telling you from my own experience; only good things have happened to me from giving up meat.

Question: Many Tibetans quote a sutra passage that says if one does not hear, see, or suspect that meat has been obtained especially for you, then it is acceptable to eat. How do you respond to this?

Rinpoche: If the animal being killed is unseen, then it is something like stealing something without being caught. That would also be deemed acceptable if you used this rationale. You could say something dirty without being heard — as if you need evidence to judge whether it is a sin or not. What they say is not right. Killing, stealing, and other negative actions can never be gotten away with. Even if other people don't see you do them, the deities, buddhas, and bodhisattvas see you doing these things. There is a Tibetan saying that even if one does not get caught committing a sin, that the gods catch you every time. It is impossible to do anything without being seen — you're always being watched by the deities. They see and understand what you did — they know that you helped to kill an animal by buying meat. This is my answer.

Question: Some monks have told me that since insects are killed in the production of rice and other vegetables, then there is really no difference in eating those things and eating meat. What do you think about this?

Rinpoche: This would mean that you wouldn't eat anything and would starve to death. If you say you were going to go for a month without killing insects through the food you eat, then you would die. If you die, this precious human life is wasted. So if you just let your body be destroyed, that means you are taking your own life, which is killing in itself. You can always take the insect from the rice when you see it and let it free outside. You don't necessarily have to kill beings to eat. Although, when we walk we crush many insects under our feet. We may not see them or observe them, but still we must be killing them. Not being aware doesn't mean that we haven't created any sin, because after all, cause and effect are always there.

After the interview, Rinpoche said to me, "Today you came to ask me these things and I answered them. It is very good. I am very happy. You have recorded my conversation, so you should relate it to the people. We are here at the place of Guru Rinpoche's cave. At this place, we are exchanging questions and answers. It will be nice for other people to hear this. When you make your book, put my interview at the beginning. Thank you."

Rinpoche's monastery at Yangleshöd has two signs posted on it related to meat eating. The first sign is in Tibetan, Nepali, and English, and is one of the first things ones sees when arriving at the monastery. The sign, a full four square meters in size, reads: IN THIS BUDDHIST MONASTERY THE CONSUMPTION OF MEAT, ALCOHOLIC BEVERAGES, & TOBACCO AS WELL AS PLAYING CARDS OR GAMBLING IS STRICTLY PRO-HIBITED.

One of the principal vows in Buddhism is to refrain from con-suming intoxicants, along with refraining from killing, stealing, lying, and sexual misconduct. Not many Tibetan Buddhists outside of the monastic tradition take this vow seriously. Rinpoche does not tolerate drinking alcohol at all among his disciples. There was an incident a few years ago where a photograph of a late lama was placed in Rinpoche's room (most likely by some disciples of this lama), and when Rinpoche saw the photo, he said, "This person was an alcoholic and had broken his precepts, don't leave his photo in my room; take it away!" The attendant removed the photo from its wooden frame, and found another photo beneath, so Rinpoche asked who was in that photo and was told it was the son of the late lama, who was also a heavy drinker. Rinpoche said, "Like father, like son. Take away both of their photos!"[54] With regard to smoking, Rinpoche has said, "The major defect of smoking is that it will close the Brahma's door at the top of one's head. So at the moment of death, it will be extremely difficult for one's practice of Phowa,[55] in trying to let one's consciousness out from there, either to liberate oneself from cyclic existence or to go to the three upper realms. It is most advisable for all Dharma practitioners — for the sake of both themselves and others — not to smoke at all!"[56]

The second sign is posted outside of the main worship area and reads in Tibetan and English, "How can we practice true compassion while we consume the flesh of an animal to fatten our own flesh? Stop this filthy habit for your health, for the environment and for the animals." This large poster placed in a protective frame was made by an animal rights group at Dzogchen Monastery in South India and shows how highly Rinpoche values this ethic.

The daughter of the great Nyingma lama Tarthang Tulku

Rinpoche, Pema, is a close friend of Chatral Rinpoche's family. In an interview conducted in 2000, she kindly offered some insights on the importance of vegetarianism with regard to Rinpoche's practice of compassion:

> Meat eating is high on Chatral Rinpoche's spiritual radar. Rinpoche is so connected with animals. He loves animals. He loves watching wildlife videos on TV. His great compassion caused him to stop eating meat. He gives all his money to save seventy truckloads of fish in Calcutta. It is his most important yearly activity. He prays for every bucket-full he dumps into the ocean, trying to bring them to a higher rebirth. In the Dharma, it is not just a matter of not doing something — eating meat for instance — but actively protecting life. Rinpoche lives this. He is so connected on a vast level to sentient beings and their suffering.
>
> Rinpoche is drawn to dark, sinful, murderous places — to Hindu animal sacrifice areas. He took his daughter Saraswati and myself to one once. It was beautiful on the outside, with flowers and carvings. He bought some birds in a cage and released them at the top of the roof. Then we came to the goat sacrifice place. At first I had my eyes closed, but then I saw it — innocent goats being murdered and blood everywhere. I was horrified. Rinpoche calmly walked over the goat blood as if he was doing walking meditation. He wasn't a bit fazed by it. I think he was trying to teach us the lesson of being fearless and patient in the face of suffering.

On Meat Eating

Meat eating is not permitted according to the three vows: the vows of individual liberation, the bodhisattva vows, and the tantric vows. Thus, Buddha stated, "I have never approved, do not approve, and will never approve of a meat diet." He declared, "My followers must never eat meat."[57]

In general, both the butcher and the buyer of meat will suffer in such realms as the burning and boiling hells.[58] In the *Lankavatara Sutra*, the Buddha taught that "killing animals for profit and buying meat are both evil deeds; these kinds of actions will result in a rebirth in the horrifying realms of hell" and "one who eats meat against the words of the Buddha is evil-minded [and is the] destroyer of the welfare of the two worlds." The Buddha further explained:

No meat can be regarded as pure if it was premeditated, asked for or desired; therefore refrain from eating meat. Both myself and other buddhas forbid adepts from eating meat. Those sentient beings who feed on one another will be reborn as carnivorous animals. The meat-eater is ill-smelling, contemptuous and born deprived of intelligence. He belongs to the lowest class of men. Since the buddhas, bodhisattvas, and *shravakas*[59] have all condemned meat eating, one who still eats meat without shame will always be devoid of sense. Those who give up eating meat will be reborn as wise and wealthy Brahmans. Meat that one has seen, heard, or suspected to have come from an animal slaughtered for meat is to be condemned. Theorizers who are born as meat-eaters will not understand this. These people will make foolish remarks about meat eating, saying, "Meat is proper to eat, unobjectionable, and permitted by the Buddha." An adept enjoys vegetarian food in appropriate quantity and views meat as unfit to eat as the flesh of one's own son. For those who are abiding in compassion, I forbid meat at all times and in all circumstances. Eating meat is a horrifying site and prevents progress towards Nirvana. Refraining from eating meat is the mark of the wise.[60]

In the *Parinirvana Sutra*, Buddha spoke to his disciple Kashyapa, saying,

> Blessed son, those who have the mindfulness of the shravakas are not allowed to eat meat from now on. Even if one is offered meat with genuine faith, one should see it as the flesh of one's own son.

Bodhisattva Kashyapa asked Buddha, "Lord, why do you not allow the eating of meat?" Buddha replied,

> Blessed son, eating meat hinders the development of compassion; therefore, all who follow the way of the Buddha should not eat meat from now on. Kashyapa, wherever a meat eater lies, sits, or walks other sentient beings become fearful upon smelling him. Blessed son, just as when a man eats garlic others will keep away because of his bad smell, likewise, when animals smell the meat eater, they fear death…

Kashyapa asked Buddha, "Lord, as monks, nuns and novice monks are dependent on other people for their food, what should they do when they are offered food with meat?" Buddha replied to Kashyapa,

> Separate the food and meat, wash the food, and then eat. You may use your begging bowl if it does not have the smell or taste of meat; otherwise you should wash the bowl. If the food has too much meat, one should not accept it. Do not eat food if you see that there is meat in it; if you do you will accumulate demerit. There will be no end if I speak thoroughly about the reasons I do not allow meat eating. I have given a brief reply because the time has come for my *parinirvana*.[61]

Buddha has further elucidated the faults of meat eating in the *Angulimala Sutra* as well as in the *Shikshasamuccaya* compendium of precepts. Furthermore, the terma teaching of Padmasambhava called *Rinchin Dronme* clearly condemns the eating of meat for both lay and ordained people: "All the followers of Buddha — monks or nuns, novice or lay — have seven main principles to follow. These are 'the four root principles'[62] and abstinence from alcohol, meat and evening food."

Although some may argue that Buddha's condemnation of meat applies only to the seven classes of Theravadayana vows[63] and is not related to the Mahayana and Vajrayana, the following Mahayana sutra passage indicates otherwise:

Meat eating is a diet that convolutes the three realms [of Samsara: the desire, form, and formless realms]. It is a sword that severs the potential for liberation. It is a fire that burns the seed of Buddhahood. It is a shaft of lightning that ends rebirth in the higher realms or a precious human rebirth.

Since meat eating is not approved for anyone — not for monks, nuns, or lay people — those who are committed Buddhist practitioners should never eat meat. One who has taken the bodhisattva vow will incur great a sin in eating the flesh of sentient beings who were one's parents in past lives. Even in the Vajrayana, meat is forbidden until one attains the ultimate view of pure perception.[64]

Trulshig Pema Dudul Rinpoche recounts a pure vision he had, after which he gave up meat forever:

The great compassionate one [Avalokiteshvara] appeared in the sky in front of me and spoke: "You have made some progress on the path and acquired some knowledge, yet you are lacking in love and compassion. Compassion is the root of the Dharma and with compassion it is impossible to eat meat. A person who eats meat will experience much suffering and illness. Look at the miserable ones! Every one is experiencing suffering according to their deeds...One who gives up meat will not experience this suffering. Instead, the buddhas and bodhisattvas, and the guru, deities, and dakinis will rejoice and protect you."

Many other renowned adepts have condemned meat as a poisonous food. Machig Labdrön, the legendary female practitioner of *chöd*,[65] said, "For me eating meat is out of the question. I feel great compassion when I see helpless animals looking up with fearful eyes." Rigzin Jigme Lingpa, a great yogi of the Nyingma tradition stated,

> Just as in the story of Arya Katayana going to beg for food,[66] I see that the animal that this meat came from was our mother in previous lives. If so, can we eat the flesh of our own mother who was slaughtered by butchers? Imagine how much concern would arise! Therefore, if we reflect honestly, there is no way we won't feel compassion for the animal.

Some people who claim to be practitioners say, "at least some meat and alcohol is necessary to keep healthy, otherwise weakness or death might come about." This is not true. However, even if death should follow from engaging in the Dharma practice of abstaining from meat and alcohol, then it is worth it. As the great adept Tsele Rigzin[67] said,

> From the bottom of my heart I pray
> Never to be with carnivores and drinkers.
> In this and lives coming
> May an ordained never be born where meat
> And alcohol are used without morality.
> Even if I should die
> Due to the absence of meat and alcohol,

I will be living in accordance with the Buddha's precepts.
Thus I will be a genuine practitioner!

Bodhisattva Orgyen Jigme Chökyi Wangpo (Patrul Rinpoche) said,

As Buddhists, we have taken the triple refuge.[68] To take refuge in the Dharma, one must practice nonviolence to sentient beings. Thus, if we continue to eat meat — which has come from the slaughtering of innocent animals — then is this not a contradiction of our Buddhist commitments?

Knowing all of the faults of meat and alcohol, I have made a commitment to give them up in front of the great Bodhi tree in Bodhgaya with the buddhas and bodhisattvas of the ten directions as my witnesses. I have also declared this moral to all my monasteries. Therefore, anyone who listens to me is requested not to transgress this crucial aspect of Buddhist ethical conduct.

Translated by Geshe Thupten Phelgye and Aaron Gross, and revised by Zach Larson.

3   The Compassionate Activity of Saving Lives

In Mahayana Buddhism, when one takes the bodhisattva vow, one pledges to work tirelessly in this life and all future lives to awaken oneself and purify oneself in order to help all other beings attain freedom from suffering through spiritual enlightenment. One vows to help beings whenever possible, and a profound way of doing this is to give a being the gift of life through an act of kindness. This can take the form of helping an animal in danger cross the road to safety before being struck by a vehicle or freeing an animal that is in captivity before it is killed by buying it from the captor and letting it roam free. If one is in a position to help save another's life — whether a human or an animal — one must practice fearless kindness to help the other being in danger.

In Tibetan Buddhism, it is believed that due to the countless incarnations all beings have undergone throughout time, at one point or another any given living creature has been one's mother in a past life. Therefore, it is viewed as an obligation to repay the kindness of those who are referred to as "mother sentient beings." If your own mother in this life were in danger, you would certainly do whatever you could to save her life. Similarly, dedicated holders of the bodhisattva vow feel this kind of urgency to save the lives of all "mother sentient beings."

Every year, Chatral Rinpoche saves the lives of tens of thousands of animals — be they insects, reptiles, mammals, birds, or fish. His most well-known activity of saving beings is his annual fish release in Calcutta, India, where seventy truckloads of fish — which have been live-caught to be sold — are purchased so that they can be released back into the ocean. Rinpoche prays for each fish, that they may one day reach the highest state of perfect Enlightenment with the help of his blessings. Not only are their lives saved, through Rinpoche's profound blessings, they are also much more likely to be reborn into a position to practice the Buddhadharma and eventually attain liberation.

In this way, Chatral Rinpoche is a quintessential bodhisattva, planting the seeds of enlightenment in all beings that are affected by him. Much like the historical Buddha himself — who through the blessings of his spoken teachings was reportedly able to instantaneously liberate frogs and other animals that overheard them — Chatral Rinpoche has the incredibly rare ability to fulfill the bodhisattva vow by doing his utmost to "bring all beings to the far shore of Nirvana."

The energy present in one's mind at the moment of death largely determines the nature of one's next incarnation. If a being is killed, the energy in their mind is likely to be fear, anger, and bewilderment — none of which are conducive to a higher rebirth. If one is rescued from this miserable end and given a chance to die naturally in a peaceful setting — in addition to having received a blessing at the moment one's life is saved — the chances are very good that the positive energy in one's mind will lead to a higher rebirth and a better chance of attaining enlightenment.

To help beings in this way, Chatral Rinpoche compiled the following prayer, entitled "Thangtong Gyalpo's Aspiration Prayer for the Liberation of Fish." It is one of the prayers he uses during his annual fish-release ceremony in Calcutta.

"Thangtong Gyalpo's Aspiration Prayer for the Liberation of Fish"

Conqueror gone to bliss, defeater of enemies, utterly pure and perfect Buddha bearing the precious *ushnisha*,[69] to you I prostrate, make offerings, and go for refuge.

If one recites this to dying animals or to other sentient beings who are on the verge of death, they will not be reborn in the lower realms. As there is such great benefit, I humbly entreat you to recite this with confident faith in the authenticity of the Buddha's word.

Infallible Three Jewels and supreme yidam,[70]
Lord of compassion, protector Avalokiteshvara,
Think of me, weak and pitiful, with loving compassion
And bear witness to the accomplishment of this vast prayer.

Long ago during the time of Buddha Chubeb
He recited the name of the bliss-gone one and liberated fish;
Likewise may I, with the rain of Dharma,
Relieve animals that are powerlessly suffering.

Some have no protector and no place to dwell,
Stricken with fear of being helplessly devoured by another,
These animals, tormented by agonizing misery,
May I relieve them with the rain of Dharma.

When they divest themselves of their present bodies,

May they avoid the lower realms

And attain the supreme happiness of gods and humans,

That they may thus listen to the holy Dharma,

Put it into practice,

And strive to achieve unexcelled Enlightenment.

I humbly ask all to recite this blessed prayer, as it is the very one the Great Siddha Thangtong Gyalpo composed while he performed the liberation of innumerable fish.

Translated by the Dzogchen Foundation.

The Benefits of Saving the Lives of Other Beings

Glory be to the Buddha Amitayus[71] and the numerous bodhisattvas!

The unimaginable benefits of such noble deeds are described in different sutras and tantras taught by Lord Buddha. The practice of such acts have been recommended by all the siddhas[72] and by both Indian and Tibetan Buddhist pandits in various scriptures. Compassion, being one of the main tenets of the Mahayana, also forms the foundation of the Theravadayana tradition, which places great emphasis on abstaining from killing or even harming any living being. The Vajrayana on the other hand has one additional facet; it lays great emphasis on maintaining a sacred bond — samaya — between the savior and the saved.

Behind all these teachings, there is one single fact of cardinal importance: that on this earth, a human being can commit no greater sin than taking the life of another living being. By implication, there is no bigger source of accumulating merit than saving life.

To obtain real peace and happiness in this world one has simply to follow the path of *ahimsa* — nonviolence — which naturally is common to all the religions of the world. If we do not like to experience any pain or suffering of any kind, how can we expect any other creature — whether big or small — to feel otherwise?

There is no better prayer or worship we can offer to Lord Buddha than being thoughtful, kind, compassionate and abstaining from taking the life of any fellow human being, animal, bird, fish or insect. Trying to save any life from imminent danger, or trying to mitigate their pain and suffering, is one step further in the active practice of loving other living beings.

The next logical step, in this regard, is saying prayers for those who die owing to some other person's thoughtless cruelty. Following this path automatically puts an end to conflicts or obstacles — if any — within our inner self, generates spontaneous happiness and bestows absolute inner peace. If your deeds flow from a genuine purity of the heart and are imbued with selflessness, they will enable you to attain enlightenment in the long run.

Conscious abstention from hunting and killing living beings, besides inspiring others to do the same, are actions behooving the kindhearted and pious. For instance, the milk of human kindness requires us to not harm migratory birds in any way, such as casting stones or nets or shooting them while they are resting for brief moments in the course of their long journey from one country or continent to another. On the contrary, we should provide help to them in all possible ways before they reach their final destination.

A renowned Buddhist scholar from Bengal, Pandit Atisha Dipankara, said that giving compassionate love to the helpless and the poor is as important as meditating on *shunyata*. The virtue of compassion is the principal foundation stone of Mahayana Buddhism.

Hence, I passionately appeal to humanity at large, irrespective of nationality, caste or religion to practice this most simple but profound virtue of compassionate love. We can praise and please our Lord Buddha in no better way than by doing all that we can to save the lives of innocent, mute, and defenseless animals, birds, fish, and insects, and thereby grant them the precious gift of life.

Moral values abjure us from taking anything that we cannot give to others. We cannot give life to anybody; it is the sole discretion of the Lord.[73] So it will be shameless arrogance and heinous sinfulness on our part if we snatch life from others.

It is my firm belief that if people adopt this practice by universal consensus, everlasting peace and all-around happiness will descend on this earth and human suffering in all its forms will become a thing of the past. All of us will become privileged enjoyers of peace, prosperity, good health, and increased longevity. In such an ideal situation, human beings will experience peace of mind and contentment of heart even at death. Bereft of any disturbing thoughts or hallucinations while being aware of the essence of the Dharma, he or she will pass away in perfect serenity and — in due course — will be reborn in higher realms. Continuous practice of this noble path will ultimately lead to the attainment of Nirvana.

May one and all follow this most meritorious path and benefit all living beings, besides accumulating a wealth of merit for themselves in the process.

MAMA KOLING SAMANTA[74]

Translated by Chowang Acharya, Senior Lecturer, Sikkim Nyingma Institute, Gangtok, Sikkim.

4 A Brief Summary of the Benefits of Building, Circumambulating, Prostrating to, and Making Aspiration Prayers at a Stupa

Homage to the Three Jewels!

I will briefly explain the benefits of building a Buddha stupa and the advantages for the faithful ones who prostrate before, make offerings to, and circumambulate it. By establishing here the perfect scriptures as witnesses, may those fortunate ones who can understand this teaching accept it with joy!

In the sutra *The Way of Distinguishing* it is said:

The Buddha told the young Brahmin Naytso,
"There are eighteen benefits of building a Tathagata stupa.
What are these eighteen?
One will be born as the child of a great king.

One will have an excellent body.

One will become very beautiful and attractive.

One will develop a very sharp intellectual capacity.

One will become widely renowned.

One will have a great entourage of servants.

One will become a leader of people.

One will be a support to others.

[One's greatness] will be expounded in the ten directions.

One will be able to extensively express whatever one wishes
in word and verse.

One will be worshipped by gods.

One will possess many riches.

One will obtain the kingdom of a universal monarch.

One will have a long life.

One's body will be like a collection of vajras.

One's body will be endowed with the major and minor
marks [of a Buddha].

One will take rebirth in the three higher realms.

One will swiftly attain complete Nirvana.

These are the eighteen benefits of building a Tathagata stupa."

In the *Manjushri Root Tantra* it is said:

If you make a stupa with your own hands,

You will be able to purify your body even if you have committed
the five inexpiable sins.[75]

If you build one hundred thousand stupas,
You will be transformed into a universal monarch of the
knowledge-holders,
Completely understand all treatises
And be endowed with skillful means.
For the duration of an eon, when you die you will always be
reborn as a king and never again go to the lower realms.
Like the sun rising in a central land,
You will be endowed with all of your sense faculties.
You will be able to retain all that you learn and remember your
past lives.

In the sutra called *Chest of Secret Relics* it is said:

The Bhagavan proclaimed,
"Vajrapani, when you write down Dharma teachings and place
them inside a stupa, that stupa will become a relic of the
vajra essence of all Tathagatas.
That stupa will be consecrated by the secret essence of all the
mantras of the Tathagatas.
It will become a stupa of ninety-nine Tathagatas, as many as a
heap of mustard seeds.
That stupa will be blessed as if it contained the eyes and ushni-
shas of all Tathagatas.
Whoever places images of the Buddha inside a stupa will
definitely be blessed by those Tathagata images with
the nature of the seven royal treasures of a universal

monarch. Whoever pays reverence and honors that stupa
Will definitely become a nonreturner[76] and will
eventually achieve the unexcelled and completely perfect
state of enlightenment — actual, full Buddhahood.
Even if one offers only one prostration or makes a single
Circumambulation, one will be altogether freed from
reaching various hell realms such as the Hell of Incessant
Torture.
One will never fall back on the path to unexcelled completely
perfect Enlightenment.
All Tathagatas will bless the entire area that surrounds the place
the stupa has been built in.

In the *Sutra of the White Lotus of the Sacred Dharma*, it says,

Walls are made from mud and bricks
And a stupa of the Victorious One is made likewise.
Therefore, even if made by a simple heap of dust in a remote
place of despair, or if a child playing games makes one
from a mound of sand,
Whomever simply builds one on the account of the Victorious One
All of them will attain enlightenment.

The benefits of making offerings to a stupa are stated in the *Sutra
Requested by King Prasenajit*:

If one applies whitewash to a Buddha stupa,

One will have a long life in the worlds of gods or humans,
One will be free of mental and physical ailments,
All suffering will be completely removed and
One will always be happy and will become wealthy with worldly
     riches.

By ringing a bell in front of a Buddha stupa,
One will speak with authority and have great fame,
One will have the pleasant voice of Brahma,
Be able to remember one's past lives,
And obtain all kinds of adornments.

If a learned person silently recites prayers on their rosary
with a faithful mind at a Buddha stupa,
They will have many golden rosaries adorned with beautiful
     precious jewels,
And will be foremost among the meritorious and fortunate ones.

Whoever makes a melodic music offering at a Buddha stupa
Will have an abundance of courageous eloquence in profundity
     and knowledge,
Their physical body will be perfect and their mind and speech
     pure.
Their voices will fill the world.

If any person who has a heart and a body,
Hangs various banners from the stupa

Which is a stainless source of merit,
It will become a field of offerings and an object of worship for
the three worlds.

If one affixes a silken crown to a Buddha stupa,
One will become a glorious ruler of humans,
A powerful ruler of gods,
Will experience great bliss and, in particular,
Will attain the crown of complete liberation.

If one cleans a Buddha stupa,
One will become very attractive and beautiful to look at,
One will have an excellent face
With the complexion of a lotus,
And one will be completely devoid
of the defects of Samsara.

Whoever cleans off the dust around a stupa
In the springtime with clean water
Will be joyfully fanned by ladies
Holding golden-handled fans.

Regarding the benefits of prostrating and circumambulating a
stupa, it is said in the *Avalokiteshvara Sutra*:

If one respectfully prostrates before a Buddha stupa,
One will become a heroic and powerful world monarch.

Protected by the armor of gold-colored symbols
One will become an authoritative teacher who will delight the
    Buddha.

In the *Sutra of the White Lotus of the Sacred Dharma*, it is said:

Whoever joins their palms together before a stupa,
Whether with both hands or just one,
Whoever briefly bows their head
Or bows their body just once,

Whoever prostrates or merely says "Buddha," even with a
    distracted mind,
Whether once or a few times
Before a stupa where relics are kept,
Will attain supreme Enlightenment.

In the *Decisive Verses on Circumambulating a Stupa*, it is said:

The excellent qualities of circumambulating
A stupa of the Buddha, Protector of the World,
Cannot be sufficiently described with mere words.

These and other quotations from the sutra and tantra scriptures
should produce great joy and confidence. I encourage all those who
aspire to happiness to make the most of their human existence. Strive
as much as you can to accumulate merit and purify obscurations by

paying homage and making offerings, circumambulating, making prayers of aspiration and so on with a noble bodhicitta motivation, to the excellent supreme foundation (stupas), which grant very meaningful benefits through seeing, hearing and remembering them.

This was composed by the renunciant Buddha Vajra, who in this time of the rampant five degenerations gives the appearance of guiding beings through the physical embodiment of the Buddha's body, speech, and mind.[77]

Composed in the Male Fire Horse Year of the sixteenth Cycle (1966) in the ninth month on the twenty-second day. May it be auspicious!

5 Helping Beings in a Degenerate Age

During one of our interviews at Yangleshöd, Chatral Rinpoche recounted the following:

Every year there is a rainy season summer retreat called Yarney. It used to be a time of year when Tibetan monks didn't travel much. It was observed primarily to avoid killing insects by walking. But now in this degenerate age, hardly any people make the effort to stay in one place for this long. We are nearing the end of an era, where people who say they are followers of the Buddha steal, commit adultery and run businesses that profit from dishonesty. They do all sorts of unrighteous things. There are some bad obstacles to the Buddhadharma and due to this people do these things they are not supposed to do. Because of this, there is a lot of war, weapons, and all sorts of negative things happening. The big nations and small nations all have disputes with each other most of the time. There is unrest everywhere. All of the negative actions are running rampant and sins are frequent. Because of that there is no timely rainfall, which leads to droughts. Natural disasters are common. Whenever someone says something it is always tinged with negativities. Those who live in peace and tranquility are being robbed. Those who are giving teachings of the holy Dharma to other people are not given the proper respect and the sacred Dharma is wasted. The situation is becoming very bad. Both outside and inside, there are disputes — among families and nations. These are the results of our past defilements, and we must take responsibility for them.

According to Tibetan Buddhist astrology, we are in "the age of residues" where only traces of the virtue of the "golden age" remain. These troubled times are marked by war, disease, natural disasters, rampant drug use and disrespect towards spirituality. Guru Padmasambhava saw all of this coming and that is why he came up with his terma system of concealing teachings to be discovered by the reincarnations of his twenty-five disciples — called *tertons* or treasure-revealers — at the appropriate time for these teachings to help the beings of that generation. Tulku Thondup explains, "[Guru Rinpoche] gave the Mind-mandate Transmission[78] of the teachings [to his core group of disciples] and recognized them as his own regents and blessed them to tame the beings of the end-age."[79] One of the most famous terma of this generation has been translated as *The Tibetan Book of the Dead* and is a guide to help beings at the moment of their death remain fearless and peaceful in the transition period between physical death and the moment when they are reincarnated again. Unprecedented times like a degenerate age require unprecedented teachings like terma.

The Dzogchen teachings of the Longchen Nyingthig, which are based on the mind terma that Rigzin Jigme Lingpa (1729–1798) received from Guru Padmasambhava, are viewed as particularly powerful in this degenerate age, as they have the potential of spontaneously liberating beings who have the proper preparation in just one lifetime. Some other teachings take many years to study before one gets a chance to practice them and it is assumed one will not be able to attain enlightenment for several lifetimes. With Dzogchen, one can put oneself in a position to practice the very highest teachings in as little as six years (in the case of Chatral Rinpoche's disciples) and if the conditions are right, one may be able to reach the highest state of realization in order to effectively help other beings do the same.

This type of practice is by no means easy and takes many years of dedicated practice. In addition, only a small minority of spiritual practitioners has the proper capacities to be able to engage in such practice. In spite of this, Dzogchen teachings have caught on in the West. The notion of "quick enlightenment" is often the draw. If one's motivation is to help other beings, then this is a positive thing. If one simply wants to experience a high state of awareness out of ego pride or in search of a "high," then this can further accelerate the decline of a degenerate age. Higher tantric teachings were not meant to be available to the general public and they can be dangerous and psychologically damaging to those who are unfit to practice them. There are more than a few Westerners who have "gone off the deep end" by engaging in practices they were not ready for.[80] Still, Dzogchen has unlimited potential to liberate beings when the conditions are right for them to practice these teachings.

Chatral Rinpoche encourages his students to approach Dzogchen the right way, by doing their *ngöndro* preliminaries, followed by a three-year retreat in which the guru can observe the disciple. After this, a three-year period where the disciple observes the guru is required. If they have proven themselves to be genuine practitioners who are completely dedicated and if their merit and wisdom are sufficient, they may then be blessed with some of the higher teachings.

One of the most terrifying developments of this degenerate age we are in has been the advent of nuclear weapons. The use of these weapons on Japan in World War II led to the most hideous forms of suffering for the people there. These weapons caused millions to fear life itself at certain points during the Cold War between the United States and the Soviet Union. With the very existence of these weapons, the possibility for heinous and senseless destruction on an unfathomable scale is still a sad reality.

Chatral Rinpoche composed the following prayer in hopes that the future will be a time of joy and not of devastation.

"A Prayer to Avert Nuclear War"

Namo Guru Ratnatraya!
To the Teacher and the Three Jewels, I bow.

True leader of the golden age — Crown of the Shakyas![81]
Second Buddha, Prince of Oddiyana, Lake-Born Vajra,[82]
Bodhisattvas, eight closest spiritual heirs,
The high noble ones, Avalokiteshvara, Manjushri, Vajrapani,[83] and
    the others!
Twenty-one Taras, Host of Noble Elders,
Root and lineage lamas, deities, peaceful and wrathful gods!
Dakinis in your three realms![84]
You who Through wisdom or karma have become defenders of the
    doctrine!
Guardians of the directions!
Seventy-five glorious protectors!
You who are clairvoyant, powerful, magical, and mighty!

Behold and ponder the beings of this time of turmoil!
We are beings born in this sorry degenerate age;
An ocean of ill effects overflows from our universally bad actions.
The forces of light flicker,
The forces of darkness — a demon army — inflame great and
    powerful men
And they rise in conflict, armed with nuclear weapons
That will disintegrate the earth.

The weapons of perverse and errant intentions
Have unleashed the hurricane.
Soon, in an instant, it will reduce the world
And all those in it to atoms of dust.

Through this ill-omened devil's tool
It is easy to see, hear, and think about
Ignorant people, caught in a net of confusion and doubt,
Who are obstinate and still refuse to understand.
It terrifies us just to hear about or to remember
This unprecedented thing.
The world is filled with uncertainty,
But there is no means of stopping it, nor place of hope,
Other than you, undeceiving Three Jewels and Three Roots.[85]
If we cry to you like children calling their mother and father,
If we implore you with this prayer,
Do not falter in your ancient vows!
Stretch out the lightning hand of compassion!
Protect and shelter us defenseless beings and free us from fear!

When the mighty barbarians sit in council of war —
Barbarians who rob the earth of joy and happiness,
Barbarians who have wrong, rough, poisonous thoughts —
Bend their chiefs and lieutenants
To the side of peace and happiness!

Pacify on the spot, the armed struggle that obstructs us!
Turn away and defeat the atomic weapons

Of the demons' messengers,
And by that power, make long the life of the righteous,
And spread the theory and practice of the doctrine
To the four corners of this great world!

Eliminate root, branch, and leaf — even the names
Of those dark forces, human and nonhuman,
Who hate others and the teaching!
Spread vast happiness and goodness
Over this fragile planet!

Elevate it truly with the four kinds of glory!
And as in the golden age, with all strife gone,
Let us be busy only with the dance of happiness,
The dance of joy!
We pray with pure thoughts
By the ocean of compassion of the three supreme refuges
And the power of the realm of truth,
The complete sublime truth,
Achieve the goal of this, our prayer
Magically, just as we have hoped and dreamed!

Translated by Richard Kohn and Lama Tsedrup Tharchin.

6   Places of Enlightenment: The Sacred Geography of Yolmo and Maratika

The Buddhism of Tibet was formed in a landscape of intense beauty and splendor. It is no wonder, then, that the physical environment became a support for internal spiritual development. This is most evident in the tradition of Dzogchen, where gazing into the sky has long been used to facilitate experiencing the vast and luminous nature of mind and meditation retreat in remote mountainous areas is emphasized.

More than one thousand years ago, Guru Padmasambhava recognized that certain areas in the Himalayan region were highly conducive to realization. He practiced extensively at some of these places, such as the Maratika cave in eastern Nepal, where he attained immortality by accomplishing the realization of Amitayus — the buddha of infinite life. He discovered others while traveling to Tibet, and wrote about them in his hidden terma texts to encourage future devotees to practice at these powerful places, such as Yolmo in northern Nepal.

The Yolmo Valley has many different aspects that are beneficial to practitioners. Ian Baker writes:

> …Chatral Rinpoche said that specific [places] in Yolmo are conducive to particular kinds of practice. Places with waterfalls inspire reflection on impermanence. Places with steep cliffs where the rocks are dark and jagged are good for meditating on wrathful deities. Places with rolling hills and flowering meadows support meditation on peaceful deities.… Chatral Rinpoche clarified that the *beyul* [hidden lands] that Padmasambhava established in Tibet are not literal arcadias, but paradises for Buddhist practice, with multiple dimensions corresponding to increasingly subtle levels of perception. Beyond Yolmo's visible terrain of mountains, streams, and forests, he said, lies an inner level, corresponding to the flow of intangible energies in the physical body. Deeper still, the subtle elements animating the environment merge with the elements present within the practitioner — the secret level. Finally, at the beyul's innermost level — *yangsang* — lies a paradisiacal, or unitary dimension revealed through an auspicious conjunction of person, place, and time . . . Chatral Rinpoche contended that yangsang is not merely a metaphor for the enlightened state, but an ever-present, if hidden, reality.[86]

Chatral Rinpoche has been guiding disciples in Yolmo for several decades, many whom engage in the traditional three-year, three-month retreat. Rinpoche wrote the following poem about Yolmo:

The mountains rise like spiked weapons towards the sun.
The mountains that lie in shadow spread like flames.
In this snow-encircled, broad sandy plain,
Padmasambhava and an assembly of realized beings,
Thinking of those in later generations,
Hid innumerable profound Dharma treasures.

All around and in every place, fragrances fill the air,
Plantains and other edible plants
Bloom in abundance without being sown,
Amiable birds, waterfowl, and wood pigeons
Empty the mind of its weariness.
Inner understanding and virtues naturally increase,
Benefiting the activity of path, view, and meditation.

For the practitioner of *rushen*[87] and chöd
There is no better place than this!
This strife-free hidden-land of Padmasambhava
Is no different than the eight great charnel grounds of India.
Surrounded by moats of water and walls of earth and rock,
Graced perpetually by clouds, mist, and rain,
[The valley] is naturally sealed [from the outer world].

If from among hundreds there are a few
Endeavoring to practice Dharma from their hearts,
I say, "Come to this place for the attainment of Buddhahood in
    this life!"
Practitioners of the inner yogas remove obstructing conditions here.
May there be spontaneous and auspicious benefit for oneself and
    others.[88]

The Maratika cave is one of the most sacred sites in the world to devotees of Padmasambhava, for it is here that he achieved immortality while accomplishing the Amitayus practices with his consort Mandarava. It is the power place that those in Chatral Rinpoche's tradition go to when engaging in longevity practices. Perhaps Chatral Rinpoche's own longevity (being healthy and active in his 90s) is a result of the time he spent practicing in Maratika.

Rinpoche wrote "The Melodious Tambura[89] of Joy" as a guide for those who are unfamiliar with the Maratika cave and who might one day have the opportunity to practice at this powerful place.

The Melodious Tambura of Joy
A Guide to the Supreme Holy Place of Immortal Life, the Rocky Cave of Maratika

Homage to the guru, yidam, and dakinis!
To the essence of all appearances, Padma Amitayus,[90]
To the embodiment of emptiness, the great mother, clothed in
white[91]
To the three-root long-life deities,[92] *the mudra of nonduality,*
I bow down with devotion and beseech you to bestow the
empowerment of immortal life.

North of Bodhgaya — the center of the universe — within a rocky mountain covered with trees and bushes, is the widely renowned wondrous holy place called Haleshi,[93] which I will now describe, so listen for a moment with joy.

Outwardly, it is the blissful play of Shiva and Umadevi.[94] Inwardly, it is the palace of Chakrasamvara.[95] Secretly, it is the celestial mansion of the deities of immortal life and most secretly, it is the Pureland of Great Bliss, the absolute realm of Akanishta.[96]

In the past, when the Vidhyadhara Pema Thödrengtsal[97] and his enchanting divine consort Mandarava engaged in the secret practice of directly entering [the mandala][98] at this place, the empowerment of immortal life was bestowed upon them by Amitayus, the buddha of infinite life. Attaining the body that is without birth or death, decrepitude or disintegration, Guru Rinpoche even now dwells in the southwest, subduing the rakshas,[99] continuously sending forth emanation after emanation in whatever way necessary to benefit beings in cyclic existence.[100]

Later, from between the eyes of Songtsen Gampo — who was Avalokiteshvara in person — the noble monk Akarma was emanated. When the noble monk Akarma was erecting a statue of the eleven-headed Avalokiteshvara in the Jokhang,[101] he went in search of special substances to make it with and relics to put inside. He miraculously arrived at Maratika and at that time saw the faces of many deities. He called it the Practice Cave "Mandala of Glorious Qualities" and uttered many other praises. This provides a reliable source and proof of Maratika's greatness.

When the heretical teacher Shankaracharya caused much harm to the Buddhist doctrine in India and Nepal, many old sacred sites and holy objects were destroyed, scattered and lost. After that, all his followers took them over as places to worship Shiva.

At the present time, people make special offerings of bell and cymbal music, tridents, one hundred or one thousand butter lamps, incense, flowers, and the three white offerings.[102] But not one person offers live sacrifice or red offerings. Their pujas, performed with the slow and fast playing of drums, cymbals, white conches, and many types of instruments of the blowing and twirling variety, cause the sounds of *ur-ur*, *chem-chem*, and so forth to resound in the cave.

They continuously make offering and praises to Brahma, Vishnu, Shiva, and other worldly deities. Adhering to their ancient traditions, they differentiate between superior and inferior castes from brahmin to butcher, and there are those who are allowed and those who are not allowed to enter the cave. Some of the inferior castes may only sit at the entrance of the cave.

Especially during the tenth of the month, the waxing and waning stages of the moon and other excellent days, I have seen brahmin priests inside the cave with mandalas of colored sand and huge fire ceremonies.

As all individuals have their own perception, it is not right to harbor wrong views and speak maligning words. One should maintain pure vision, rejoice, and give praise — thus making a good connection. To slander other people or their deities is the basis for misfortune.

To arouse interest and develop faith in outsiders — Buddhists and ordinary people — and to dispel arguments about this holy place at the same time, I began with an explanation of the history of Maratika.

EMA![103] Having mentioned some of the qualities of this holy place, which are clearly evident even to ordinary people, there can hardly be room for disagreement. In addition, it is said in the commentaries, with good reason, that even the words of a child — if authentic and well-spoken — should suffice in describing such a place.

On seeing this place, boundless wonder arises. Through merely hearing the name, the seed of liberation is planted. By recalling it, accidental death is prevented. Through making prostrations, circumambulation and offerings, great accumulation of merit is accomplished.

The sky around it forms a vast eight-spoked wheel. The ground is shaped like an eight-petalled lotus with the middle swelling up like the flower's pistil. The landscape being wide and open, the sun remains for a long time and the weather is temperate. In the front, a stream gushes forth. The center of the holy place is a huge self-existing assembly hall, high and spacious with room for one thousand people. There is a single skylight in the center shaped like a round wheel.

Outside, various shrubs and trees grow out of the craggy rocks. Inside the cave, innumerable images of statues, seed-syllables and hand implements of the peaceful and wrathful deities abound. The unique characteristic of this holy place is the many stone lingam (stalagmites) ranging in size from six feet to six inches. Naturally formed, they are white, smooth, shiny and resplendent.

During auspicious times, nectar collects like moist dew and drips down. There are many crevice-like holes through which one can test one's positive or negative karma to see whether one is headed for a birth in the lower realms or to the higher realms and the path of liberation.

Below this holy place is a cave whose entrance faces to the southwest. The mouth of the cave is not so big, but once inside it opens up and is very wide and spacious, with enough room to fit a hundred people. There are many symbols of the body, speech and mind of the enlightened ones as well as hand and foot imprints, a white conch and many other amazing self-arisen things. When those of fortunate karma arrive there, dew-like nectar seeps out. Straight above, unobstructed, is a high vaulted skylight, making it renowned as a training place for the practice of transferring one's consciousness to a Pureland.

In the spacious expanse of the main cave are hosts of bats who you can't see but who ceaselessly make the sound of the mantra of long life (one hears the sounds of *tsey* and *bhrum*).

For all tantric practitioners who have entered the path, it is a very good place for the practice of visualizing a luminous wheel of deities and mantras.

This text, which mentions only a drop from the ocean of good qualities of this holy place, was composed with the thought of benefiting others. Like a wish-fulfilling gem or an excellent vase, may it unfailingly bring all our wishes to fruition.

Having been introduced to this sacred place, it is certain that we Dharma brothers and sisters who follow Guru Padmasambhava will accumulate merit and purify obscurations by engaging in the recitation of mantras, the offering of tormas, the performing of fire ceremonies and especially the practices of longevity here.

By the merit of composing this,
May all beings under the sky be saved from untimely death and
    present obstacles
And ultimately, having attained the level of the protector Amitayus,
Lead all beings to that state.

By the blessings and power of the truth
And the wondrous compassion of the buddhas and bodhisattvas,
Removing all harmful and disadvantageous circumstances
    without exception,
May we reside in continuous glory
And may each day and night be auspicious.

My daughter Saraswasti Devi, bestowing offerings of a stainless scarf and writing paper, requested me to write a praise of this holy place. Therefore, I, the old vagabond father Sangye Dorje, wrote this in the Fire Tiger Year on an excellent day of the tenth month, between sessions, at the supreme holy place of Maratika, which puts an end to death. SHUBHAM.

7 Dudjom Rinpoche: A Master–Disciple Relationship Comes Full Circle

His Holiness Dudjom Jigdral Yeshe Dorje Rinpoche (1904–87) was one of the most brilliant teachers, scholars, and writers of all time. He received every single teaching and empowerment of the Nyingma tradition, and took it upon himself to revise and update the Nyingma Canon in order to preserve it for future generations. He composed a thorough history of the Nyingma tradition and wrote poems so potent, they have the ability to liberate fortunate beings on the spot. It is safe to say that without Dudjom Rinpoche's skillful means and compassion, the liberating teachings of the Nyingma tradition would not be flourishing outside of Tibet like they are today.

When the Sun set in the West — when Dudjom Rinpoche passed away in France in 1987 — the Moon was there to rise in the East. Chatral Rinpoche, as the Vajra Regent of Dudjom Rinpoche's tradition, is still shining brightly today, illuminating the ignorance of all beings who come into contact with him and guiding them on the path to enlightenment.

Dudjom Rinpoche entrusted Chatral Rinpoche to be his Regent for good reason, knowing that Rinpoche would flawlessly preserve his Dharma teaching lineages, such as the Dudjom Tersar, until the point when the next reincarnation of Dudjom Rinpoche was fully trained and ready to benefit beings as before. In the meantime, Chatral Rinpoche has protected those powerful teachings and only passed them on to those disciples who can truly benefit from them.

Chatral Rinpoche wrote the following prayer in 1987 to facilitate the swift rebirth of his teacher, Dudjom Rinpoche.

"The Bestower of the Glorious Fruits of Aspiration"

OM SVASTI

Yeshe Dorje, the Dharmakaya free from elaboration,
Dechen Dorje, the Sambhogakaya endowed with the fivefold
    certainties,[104]
Drodul Lingpa, the Nirmanakaya appearing as appropriate to tame
    all beings,
Are indivisible in the Lama.
To you we are calling; please look on us with compassion.

Oh Lord, having directly attained the primordial buddhahood,
You have transcended the conceptual phenomena of birth and
    death
But in the perception of your disciples, your illusory body of relative
    truth
Has dissolved into the ultimate expanse of great peace.

For all beings and doctrines in general and especially for the Early
    Translation School,
The sun of learning and practice of the oral and treasure teachings
    has turned west toward the water goddess.
We, the masses of disciples who follow you
Are left helpless with no protection and no refuge.
Please take notice!

Hence, we pray that your immaculate, supreme mind
Perfect the intrinsic clarity of inner space, the youthful vase body,
And that your magical display within the unified state of no-more-
   training,
Be swiftly manifested through a faultless emanation, the full moon
   of your rebirth.

With the five auspicious visions,[105]
By perfecting the amazing lives of the thousand buddhas
And completing enlightened activity in its entirety,
Please pervade the great, vast land of the Jambu continent.[106]

We pray that his marvelous emanation will be victorious
Over the outer and inner obstacles
And the battles with the forces of Mara,
That the wisdom, compassion, and power of the three
   bodhisattvas[107] will be clearly evident in him,
And that he will be endowed with the longevity of Buddha
   Amitayus.

We pray that by the unfolding of the excellent qualities of study,
   contemplation, and meditation,
And by the marvelous three spheres of activity[108]
That he eliminate the deteriorations due to the five
   degenerations,[109]
Rekindle the doctrine of the nine yanas,[110]
And remain as a spiritual friend, blooming the lotus of happiness
   and benefit.

By the blessings of the guru, deities, and dakinis
And by the power of the oceanlike gathering of Vajrayana
    Dharma-protectors
May this prayer and aspiration swiftly come to fruition
And may all hopes and wishes auspiciously be fulfilled.

This prayer for the Swift Return of the Manifestation, entitled "The Bestower of the Glorious Fruits of Aspiration" is prayed with strong devotion on the completion of the first phase of the waning of the moon of the eleventh month of Fire Tiger year (January 19, 1987), by Sangye Dorje, the lowest of the disciples of the Terton, near Yangleshöd, the place of accomplishments, at the earnest and undeniable requests made by sacred vajra-friends: lamas, tulkus, monks, and patrons who are the residents of Boudhanath, with presents of auspicious substances and many rupees of glorious Nepal, when the mind of the unrepayably kind lord and protector — Dudjom Jigdral Yeshe Dorje Rinpoche — entered into the ultimate expanse of great peace (on January 17, 1987). By the blessings of the gurus, buddhas, and bodhisattvas, may the prayer be granted.

"Prayer to Dudjom Yangsi Rinpoche"

Chatral Rinpoche's prayer was answered in 1990 with the birth of Dudjom Yangsi Rinpoche in Tibet, who is the son of the previous Dudjom's son Dola Rinpoche. Chatral Rinpoche was notified of the evidence that Dudjom Rinpoche had reincarnated and he confirmed that the child was indeed Dudjom Yangsi. Chatral Rinpoche consulted with Dudjom Rinpoche's son Thinley Norbu Rinpoche in New York to verify the decision, and Thinley Norbu concurred.

Chatral Rinpoche wrote the following prayer to give Dudjom Yangsi his name, Sangye Pema Shaypa Drodul Rigdzin Thrinley Drupadey. Each part of the name is included in the prayer (as indicated in boldface type).

> Atop the thousand petals of loving kindness of the **lotus** of
>   **awakening**,
> A wondrous emanation has **blossomed forth** from the pistil
> And taken a form without peer to be a regent of the Buddha, a
>   **tamer of beings**.
> He appears because of the abundant merit of his fortunate disciples.
> The culmination of **awareness holder**s, possessing vajra body,
>   speech, and mind,
> A wish-fulfilling Lord.
> Through your effortless **enlightened activity**, you bestow
>   whatever one may desire,
> Fulfilling the aspirations of all living beings in the three planes of
>   existence.[111]

Chatral Rinpoche at age 25—
a legend in the making

Kalu Rinpoche

Khenpo
Ngawang
Palzang

Jamyang
Khyentse
Chökyi
Lodrö

With
Dudjom
Rinpoche
and Dilgo
Khyentse
Rinpoche

Chatral Rinpoche
traveled exclusively
on foot

Performing the
consecration
of a stupa

Chatral Rinpoche with Father Thomas Merton

With Dudjom
Rinpoche

Chatral Rinpoche with his wife, daughters, and granddaughter, above. Below, with his granddaughter.

The Manifestation of Guru Padmasambhava's mind

Chatral Rinpoche, a yogi without peer

With the crown of Terton Dudul Dorje

Relaxing in the sky-like nature of mind at a picnic

Above, with his personal physician.
Below, Rinpoche is a holder of numerous lineages.

With Kathok Situ Rinpoche and Dudjom Yangsi Rinpoche from Tibet, two of his main disciples

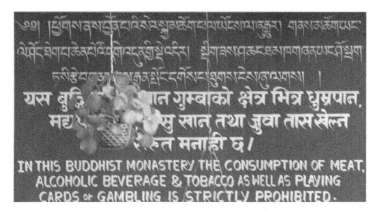

ༀ༅། སྤྱོགས་ནས་... ...ནས་མཆོད་ཡང་། ...

यस बुद्ध ... ...न गुम्बाको क्षेत्र भित्र धुम्रपान,
मद्य ... ...सु खान तथा जुवा तास खेल्न
... ...रूत मनाही छ।

IN THIS BUDDHIST MONASTERY THE CONSUMPTION OF MEAT,
ALCOHOLIC BEVERAGE & TOBACCO AS WELL AS PLAYING
CARDS or GAMBLING IS STRICTLY PROHIBITED.

Above, sign prominently posted at Rigzin Drubpe Ghatsal
Monastery. Below, Chatral Rinpoche, a heart of pure love.

Fish swim freely in a pond below Rigzin Drubpe Ghatsal Monastery as the reflection of prayer flags hanging in trees give them blessings

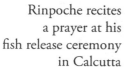

Rinpoche recites a prayer at his fish release ceremony in Calcutta

A Bodhisattva
who sees all

At the Mahabodhi
Stupa at Bodhgaya

A man of peace

Presiding over a
funeral service

In the **everlasting** essence, I pray, that you will live long.

Through the power of the truth of the oceanic Three Jewels and
Three Roots

And through the power and strength of the five **classes** of male
and female oath-bound ones,

May the aspirations of ourselves and others spontaneously reach
fruition.

And may the great undertaking of benefiting the Dharma and all
beings blaze forth!

*At Shayu Do, in the region of Kham, the child born in the family of the
supreme spiritual master Tulku Jigmed Chökyi Nyima has been unmistakably recognized as the third Dudjom Rinpoche, the reincarnation of
the Lord of Refuge Dudjom Jigdral Yeshe Dorje Rinpoche. Since many
nonsectarian figures who are well-known throughout the Ancient and
New Schools have unanimously confirmed the prophecies and signs, I
am certain that it is true. Therefore, I, Sangye Dorje — the foolish, least
worthy servant of the last incarnation of this master — have carelessly
written this long life prayer in a few words related to the offering of a
name. May it be virtuous!*

In 1994, Chatral Rinpoche presided over the enthronement ceremony of Dudjom Yangsi Rinpoche in Godavari, Nepal with about
twelve thousand people, including many of the high lamas of the
Nyingma tradition, in attendance. Since that time, he has served as
Dudjom Yangsi Rinpoche's root guru, responsible for overseeing his
education and spiritual development. The infallible relationship they

share, which has spanned more than sixty years and two incarnations, has effectively preserved the potent elixir of liberating Dharma teachings for the benefit of all sentient beings to come.

8 Advice for Nyingma Practitioners

Spoken by Chatral Rinpoche for the
2000 Nyingma Monlam Chenmo Festival

Since I am the eldest of the Nyingma lamas, I have been asked to share some humble thoughts and opinions with all those who have gathered here this year in the sacred place of Bodhgaya, India on the occasion of the Eleventh Annual Great Prayer Festival of the Early Translation School. I will therefore speak a few words of advice to express my point of view, so I hope you all listen well.[112]

First of all, I greatly rejoice that by the kindness of many bene-factors and volunteers, the Great Nyingma Prayer Festival has been taking place for many years and I myself — an old man — was able to attend it for the first three years.

Now, since we are all followers of the Buddha, we should know that taking meat and alcohol is very bad. This is one of the main things we should abandon. So the fact that everyone has agreed that

79

we will refrain from meat and alcohol [during the Great Prayer Festival] and realized that there is simply no need for us to take these things is a result of the buddhas' compassion.[113]

Some of you have a lot of responsibilities and things to look after — such as taking care of your wife and children — and in reality are therefore unable to accomplish great deeds for the benefit of the Buddha's Teachings.

As for the excellent tradition of the Great Nyingma Prayer Festival, it has been established in general to restore, preserve and expand the teachings of Lord Buddha and in particular those of the luminous Vajrayana tradition of the Early Translation School, which is endowed with the special sixfold greatness.[114] One should not mix the Dharma with worldly affairs because this Festival has been established for the sole purpose of the Dharma. Therefore, if we allow these two to get mixed up together, it is like putting fire and water in the same vessel. If the fire is very strong, the water will dry up. If the water predominates, the fire will die. So don't get mixed up with politics.[115]

Above all, what do we need to develop bodhicitta?[116] Have not all the beings of the six realms — having passed through the *bardo*[117] and been reincarnated many times — at one point been our mother and father? By following over and over the path of the Mahayana taught by the Buddha, all temporary and ultimate subtle and gross suffering will be mollified for everyone. The temporary and ultimate benefits of happiness and goodness will increase further and further.

These days we are living in the age of the five degenerations,[118] also called the "five insurmountables." In this wild and unruly time, because of such things as the proliferation of many kinds of evil weapons and the spread of different kinds of poisonous drugs such as tobacco, the Buddha's teachings are being taken away as if by an untimely frost. From all angles the explanation and practice of these precious teachings have many obstacles. Favorable conditions are few. It is like a pond that has lost its water through drought or a butter lamp that has run out of oil. Everyone knows and understands that it has come to be like this. So, to focus on restoring these teachings is what we mean here by "contributing to world peace." Apart from that, you can't simply take "peace" from one country and export it to another one. Each country or state has one person as the leader of that country or state. Different types of dark forces have transformed the minds of all of these people and they view their neighbors with prejudice; the small ones view the big ones with envy, the big ones treat the small ones with contempt and equal-size ones see each other as being competitors. Because of such biases, they engage in all kinds of wars. Even if the country we live in has peace today, in each country war will eventually be fought. These conflicts are as numerous as the grass that grows in a summer meadow or the bright stars that come out at night once the sun goes down. This is something tangible that we can see with our own eyes. So it is in order to pacify these hostilities that we recite prayers of aspiration.

The prayers that we are using in this Festival are "Reciting the Names of Manjushri"[119] — which is the quintessence of both the sutras and the tantras — and "The King of All Aspirations,"[120] which is the main prayer according to the sutras. These teachings have the complete meaning of both sutra and tantra in them. Along with them, we also recite *The Treasure of Blessing: A Sadhana of the Buddha*[121] and conclude each day with a prayer that the teachings of the Nyingma Tradition may flourish called "The Words That Rejoice the Dharma King," both composed by Jamgon Mipham Rinpoche (1846–1912). These are prayers that all of us should include in our daily practice. If that isn't possible, we should at least not fail to recite them on the tenth and twenty-fifth days of the lunar month.

It would be wrong to say, as some do, that if we don't recite prayers while being aware of their meaning and merely repeat the words mindlessly, it has no benefit whatsoever — like prayer flags flapping in the wind. However, there are indeed differences in the level of benefits and blessings derived from prayers according to the way we recite them. Therefore, keeping this in mind, at the beginning of the practice, generate bodhicitta. During the main practice, some will use an object of concentration and some will practice without an object of concentration; each person should do what is best according to their level. At the end, one should dedicate the merit in a way that is pure from the three conceptual spheres[122] to the best of one's ability. The most important and essential thing in making this Great Prayer Festival meaningful is to depend on those three stages of practice — generation of bodhicitta, the main practice and dedication of merit. All must do the complete three stages of practice.

Especially because we follow the teachings of the Nyingma Early Translation School, in the area of the view, conduct must not get lost and in the area of conduct, the view must not get lost. As Guru Rinpoche said,

In the direction of the view, if conduct gets lost, the view goes to the tarnished state of Mara.[123] In the direction of conduct, if the view is lost, having become entangled by the hopes and fears of materialism and ideology, real liberation will never come and there is no way you can reach the level of the unified state.[124]

This should be understood. Lamas, tulkus,[125] and khenpos[126] have studied many texts and know and understand this, so there is no need for me to remind them further.

These days in our Nyingma Tradition, philosophical colleges and retreat centers are spreading everywhere. What I have said thus far is no different than what the teachers explain in those centers and what the students listen to. As a result of our training, we are participating in this large gathering at Bodhgaya during the twelfth lunar month — the eighteenth day of this month being the anniversary of the passing of the all-knowing Longchen Rabjam.[127] Before that day comes — from the first to the tenth — we strive to perfect the accumulations [of merit and wisdom] and purify obscurations.

Many devotees who have faith in the Three Jewels and, especially in this Great Prayer Festival of the Early Translation School of the secret Mantrayana, have made offerings for the benefit of those who have died, for those who are helpless and without a protector and for all living beings. Fellow devotees who are in a position to receive these offerings have accepted them. These religious offerings made for the sole purpose of helping the dead and the living are not something that should be taken lightly.[128] Pondering the significance of these religious offerings, all of you must do dedication prayers and make pure aspirations for the sake of the deceased.

For the benefit of the living, we serve them with a protective prayer ritual for the sake of long life and prosperity according to their respective inner wishes. After consulting with the astrologers and doing divination, when the list of prayers to recite in the puja[129] to help that person is announced, make sure you perform the service correctly. It won't be beneficial if you don't chant the prayers and say the dedication, leaving only us to enjoy the faith offerings. This will mature as a heavy karmic burden! We must purposefully take on this great responsibility and put a seal on the practice by doing the aspiration and dedication prayers. If you put a drop of water into the ocean, until the ocean dries up, the drop of water isn't going to dry up. Similarly, by virtue of putting a seal on the practice through dedication prayers, the benefits of the practice will not rot or decay until you achieve Buddhahood. It is the Buddha's wish that this virtue not be wasted; it is the real essence of the flawless teachings of the Buddhist pandits. Everyone having understood this well; engage in the complete three stages of practice.

Now however, in terms of conduct, it is said Nyingma monks fight with and hit people. Nyingma monks don't keep their vows or samaya.[130] Nyingma monks engage in theft. When I heard this it was like thorns piercing my heart. We old lamas worry and feel responsible for this. Make sure that this type of behavior decreases every year. The leaders must take responsibility for putting a stop to this. In humility, all disciples should follow these lessons of us elders. Young ones listening to this, you must gain mastery over your own body, speech, and mind and make sure there is nothing lacking in your discipline.[131]

At a sacred place and special event like this when there is an oceanlike gathering of people, several of the great holy masters will be among them. Whoever of these great masters might be present, they should give advice like I am doing and everyone should respect and follow their advice. If you do this, imagine the manner in which the splendor of the teachings of the Nyingma Early Translation School will develop above and beyond what it is now. If you don't do this and try to pass on your responsibility to others, they will be disregarded and people won't listen. Even though some have the ability to teach, they don't use that ability. Other people either don't know or understand very little of the meaning of the teachings and say things unnecessarily.

There are a few who think that they don't need to explain general points to others because they are not interested or cannot bear to take on great responsibilities. I think this is wrong. Those who have responsibilities should advise those who don't, encouraging them to work on their discipline so it will improve year after year and become firm. If you place one being at a time on the path of discipline, thinking they will stay firmly on this path for at least one hundred years, then as long as the Buddhadharma remains, there will be harmony in the monastery with good clean discipline and no reason for others to criticize or judge. Nyingmapas and all other religious traditions have their own respective rules on discipline. Each must take responsibility for their own situation. The Nyingmapas cannot take responsibility for the other traditions — it can't be done.

Each of us Nyingmapas have either come from the three provinces, the upper, lower, and middle regions of Tibet, or been born in the noble land of India, Nepal, or anywhere in the Himalayan range east of Ladakh. There are hundreds of Nyingma monasteries — large and small — in those areas. In these monasteries, what is known as the Sangha — the monastic community — should distinguish between what is to be accomplished and what is to be avoided according to the threefold training[132] and the Statements of the Tripitaka.[133] By doing this, the so-called "noble Sangha" will be the same in both name and meaning. As it is said: "There is no guide like the Buddha. There is no protector like the Dharma. There is no fertile field[134] like the Sangha. One should always rely on those three." While saying that, you should also understand that, as a leading figure of the Three Jewels, the Sangha needs to engage seriously in the teachings of the Buddha and encourage others to do so. This is what is meant by being "holders of the Teachings."

Apart from that, even if one is a fortunate businessman — no matter how well they did in amassing great wealth — a mansion itself will not make one a holder of the Buddhadharma. The nature of one's clothing will also not make one a holder of the teachings. Even wearing monk's robes will not make one a holder of the teachings. In reality though, even if a person is a lowly beggar, if they are in harmony with the Dharma they can be called a great person who is a holder of the teachings.

If you don't become like this, even if one thinks they are a holder of the teachings by being in various positions like the head of a sitting row[135] or sitting exclusively on an exalted throne, it is a difficult thing if they may have a correction coming as to whether or not they are a holder of the teachings based on how they live. If one speaks purely in accordance with the Dharma, it might offend a few. If what I say is wrong, please forgive me. I openly confess it. It is my misunderstanding. It is a mistake. It is a distortion. It is lack of knowledge. If it may have also just been the phony advice of an old man, I don't know. As an old man saying these things, I am just proclaiming all the thoughts in my mind. It is possible that it is like this — that there was no need for me to discuss these things — that I am discussing that which I don't have reason to discuss and saying that which I don't have reason to say. All people will come to make mistakes like this — not just me.

Everyone said that there was a need for some spoken advice for this year's Great Prayer Festival. So, [Penor Rinpoche's attendant] Kunsang Lama was sent to me and came to Yangleshöd. At that time, I had been very busy satisfying some benefactors elsewhere in the Kathmandu Valley and while being in a great hurry I came to Yangleshöd. As soon as I had gotten out of the car, I spontaneously spoke this advice and did not have time to consult texts or write it down. There was no need to do so anyway. I don't expect it to be on the shelf of a Buddhist philosophical college library. For this year alone, it was suggested that among us elder Nyingma lamas, someone should explain how discipline should be kept. That was the opinion of others and I also think that this is right. Other lamas would not feel comfortable listening to the advice of someone who is unknown, so that is why one who is known as a "lama" like myself is speaking out.

Lamas, tulkus, and khenpos who are knowledgeable are qualified to give advice and should do so. Otherwise, those who just say things in the way of meaningless gossip and talk nonsense will just create conflicts. There is no benefit whatsoever in saying things that will only go on to increase our attachment, anger and delusion. Talking in this way will harm the Buddha's teachings and be of help to no one.

For the benefit of all beings, all the practitioners of the teachings of the Nyingma Early Translation School living in monasteries great or small, from Upper, Middle or Lower Tibet, in a mountain hermitage, a study center with just four monks or even if you are practicing alone; for all of you year after year when you gather here again at this time, you must take responsibility for upholding your discipline. For the period of these ten days, if you don't have something good to say, there is no reason for you to speak. You should behave in such a way that no one will have reason to criticize or gossip about your conduct so that you can be a perfect example to lead the faithful and become worthy objects of the accumulation of merit of the benefactors.

I hope and pray that this event will come to be very good through the planning at the beginning, middle and end. It will then serve to benefit the longevity of the great holy beings who hold the teachings of the Dharma. In the long term, it will also help the Buddha's precious teachings by way of the two *chakras*[136] of teaching and practice to never fade and instead expand and flourish now and always in the four times[137] and ten directions and abide for a long time.

During this degenerate age in the outer world, there are many natural disasters due to the upsetting of the four elements.[138] Also, demonic forces come with their many weapons to incite the fighting of wars. All of those forces have caused the world to come to ruin and led all to tremble with fear — so terrified that their hair stands up on end. Still, the demonic forces find it necessary to come up with many new types of weapons. If we were called on to confront them, there's no way we Dharma practitioners could defeat them. That's why we make supplication prayers to the Three Jewels, do the aspiration prayers, the offering prayers and the prayers of invocation. We are responsible for those activities. This is what I urge you to do. So at this great gathering, please think about the pacification of all these forces.

Since I don't think there is anything inconsiderate or unacceptable in this advice, please listen to it carefully and take it to heart. If you do so, when the Great Prayer Festival is over, you will have good reason to be happy and will be able to rejoice in the merit you have accumulated. So please make it happen that way! May you have a long life! Please — all of you — make vast prayers of aspiration so that the precious teachings of the Victorious One may flourish in the ten directions. That's about all that an old man like me has to say. May you all keep this advice in your minds.

This oral advice was recorded and transcribed in 2000 and translated from the Tibetan by Zach Larson with the assistance of Tsetan Chonjore and Thinley Dhondrup in 2004.

9 Words of Advice

Namo Gurubhyah[139]

Precious master of unrepayable kindness, Pema Ledrel Tsal,[140]
I pray that you remain as the crown ornament on the top of my
     head.
Grant your blessings so that we may find freedom here and now
From all the sufferings of samsara and its lower realms!

Listen well, my dear disciples who are gathered here.
For all those whose hearts have not been spoiled, consider this:

The chances of finding a human existence are one in a hundred.
Now that you have found one, if you fail to practice the sublime
     Dharma,
How could you possibly expect to find such an opportunity again?
This is why it is crucial that you take advantage of your situation.

Conceiving of your body as a servant or a thing to ferry you about,
Do not allow it to rest in idleness for even a single moment;
Use it well, spurring on your entire body, speech, and mind to
    virtue.

You might spend your whole life in pursuit of only food and
    clothing,
With great effort and without regard for suffering or harmful deeds,
But when you die you cannot take even a single thing with you
    — consider this well.
The clothing and alms needed to keep you alive are all you need.
You might dine on the finest meal of delicious meat and alcohol,
But it all turns into something impure the very next morning,
And there is nothing more to it than that.
So be content with life-sustaining provisions and simple clothes,
And be a loser when it comes to food, clothing, and conversation.

If you do not reflect on death and impermanence,
There will be no way to practice Dharma purely,
Practice will remain an aspiration, one that is constantly postponed,
And you may feel regret the day that death comes, but by then it
    will be too late!

There is no real happiness among any of the six classes of beings,
But if we consider the sufferings of the three lower realms,
Then, when you feel upset just by hearing about them,
How will you possibly cope when you experience them directly?

Even the happiness and pleasures of the three upper realms
Are just like fine food that has been laced with poison —
Enjoyable at first, but in the long run a cause of ruin.

What's more, all these experiences of pleasure and pain
Are not brought about by anyone but yourself.
They are produced by your own actions, good and bad.
Once you know this, it is crucial that you act accordingly,
Without confusing what should be adopted and abandoned.[141]

It is far better to eliminate your doubts and misconceptions
By relying on the instructions of your own qualified teacher,
Than to receive many different teachings and never take them any
    further.

You might remain in a solitary place, physically isolated from the
    world,
Yet fail to let go of ordinary concerns and, with attachment and
    aversion,
Seek to bring defeat upon your enemies while furthering the
    interests of your friends,
And involve yourself in all kinds of projects and financial dealings.
There could hardly be anything worse than that.

If you lack the true wealth of contentment of mind,
You will think you need all kinds of useless things,
And end up even worse than an ordinary person,

Because you won't manage even a single session of practice.
So set your mind on freedom from wanting anything at all.
Wealth, success, and status are simply ways of attracting enemies
    and demons.
Pleasure-seeking practitioners who fail to turn their minds from this
    life's concerns
Sever their connection to the authentic Dharma.

Take care to avoid becoming stubbornly impervious to the
    teachings.
Limit yourself to just a few activities and undertake them all with
    diligence.
Not allowing your mind to become fidgety and restless,
Make yourself comfortable on your seat in a retreat cabin.
This is the surest way to gain the riches of a Dharma practitioner.

You might remain sealed in strict retreat for months or even years,
But if you fail to make any progress in the state of your mind,
Later, when you tell everyone about all that you did over such a long
    time,
Aren't you just bragging about all your hardships and destitution?
All their praise and acknowledgments will only make you proud.

To bear mistreatment from our enemies is the best form of austerity,
But those who hate criticism and are attached to compliments,
Who take great pains to discover all the faults of others,
While failing to keep proper guard over their own mindstream,

And who are always irritable and short-tempered,
Are certain to bring breaches of samaya upon all their associates,
So rely constantly on mindfulness, vigilance, and conscientiousness.

No matter where you stay, be it a busy place or a solitary retreat,
The only things that you need to conquer are mind's five poisons[142]
And your own true enemies, the eight worldly concerns,
Nothing else.
Whether it is by avoiding them, transforming them, taking them as
   the path, or looking into their very essence,
Whichever method is best suited to your own capacity.

There is no better sign of accomplishment than a disciplined mind.
This is true victory for the warrior who carries no weapons.
When you practice the teachings of the sutras and tantras,
The altruistic bodhicitta of aspiration and application is crucial,
Because it lies at the very root of the Mahayana.
Just to have this is enough, but without it, all is lost.

*These words of advice were spoken in the hidden grove of Padma, in
the place called Kunzang Chöling, in the upper hermitage in a forest
clearing, by the old beggar Sangye Dorje. May it be virtuous!*

Translated by Adam Pearcey, Lotsawahouse.org

"Prayers for the Long Life of Chatral Rinpoche"

OM SVASTI

By the compassion and the power of the aspirations of
    the Guru of Uddiyana[143] and his retinue,
You have taken the excellent birth of Sangye Dorje, the spiritual hero;
May your lotus feet remain firm for hundreds of eons.
May the great undertaking of taming beings and your enlightened
    activity flourish and reach its ultimate goal!

Written by Chatral Rinpoche at the request of Wangchen Palmo.
Translated by Zach Larson.

In particular, may you, the magical display of Guru
    Padmasambhava's mind,
Be victorious in the battle with the incorrigible wrong views of the
    Dark Age
And increase even further the Dharma's reaches to fulfill our aims.
May your life last for one hundred years,
Blazing with the virtuous marks that spontaneously accomplish the
    two benefits,[144]
So that the sound of the secret teachings pervades through the three
    worlds![145]

Written by Dudjom Rinpoche. Translated by Erik Pema Kunsang.

OM SVASTI

The great blissful all-pervading awareness-emptiness, the absolute
    deity
Endowed with the indestructible seven aspects of integration and
    boundless life,
Assembly of realized immortal Vidyadaras,
Here and now, confer the glory of accomplishment upon these
    words of truth.

Samantabhadra, primordially free from destruction and dissolution,
The ultimate guide, supreme innate natural awareness,
By the oceanlike gathering of the inseparable Three Roots
At this moment, send abundant blessings of indestructible
    realization.
On the ground of perfect equanimity, the unmoved primordial
    purity,
Free from hopes and fears, grasping and grasped,
The extraordinary body, speech and mind
Are completed in the essence of perfect permanence, free from death
    and transformation,
Ripening into maturity as the absolute, immortal, innate state.

In the supreme display of the gesture of effortless bliss and
    emptiness,
He rules all in the form of a spontaneously perfect, fearless spiritual
    hero.

May he live long, free from decline and repeated births and deaths,
May he not leave us, but continually remain firm as the essence of
    the Dharmakaya,
Appearing in unimaginable forms to his disciples, myself and others.
Complete with the major and minor marks, the great mandala of
    accomplishment,
May he live in the essence of boundless longevity.
And may he always guide us and nurture us with his wisdom mind.

*This request for my glorious root lama, possessing great kindness, to have a
long life and remain firm for hundreds of eons so that the Dharma wheel
may be turned uninterruptedly for myself and other disciples was written
on the morning of the fifteenth day of the third Tibetan month in the
Bird Year by the very lowest of his disciples, the one who is called Shyalpa
Jigme Tenzin Wangpo.*

OM SVASTI

The glorious Lord of Refuge, Chatral Sangye Dorje,
Whose body is Vajrasattva, resplendent with pure light, blessing all
    those who are in his presence;
Whose speech is Samantabhadra,[146] containing the sublime Truth
    of Dharmakaya and the liberating teachings of Dzogpa Chenpo;
Whose mind is Guru Padmasambhava, subduing negative forces
    and taming the beings of this degenerate age;
Whose qualities are equal to that of all the buddhas of past, present
    and future;

Whose activity is Avalokiteshvara, manifesting wherever he is
　　needed to bring beings on the path of enlightenment with
　　boundless compassion;
Please continue to bless us with your enlightened presence until all
　　beings reside in the blissful state beyond suffering;
May your life be secure and without obstacle for as long as sentient
　　beings remain in Samsara and endlessly tranquil thereafter;
May the noble view of supreme bodhicitta[147] that you represent
　　manifest in all beings spontaneously and effortlessly like an
　　infinite field of lotuses in full bloom.

*This prayer was written on the twenty-ninth day of October, 2004 with
great devotion and aspiration by the lay practitioner Ngawang Yönten in
the place of Guru Padmasambhava's cave, Yangleshöd, Nepal. May it be
virtuous!*

Dedication of Merit

Through this merit,[148] may all beings attain the level that transcends the limitations of Samsara and Nirvana.

By defeating the armies of Mara, may they masterfully acquire the great kingdom of Samantabhadra.

May the two benefits spontaneously manifest and may auspiciousness and splendor blaze forth.

Appendix I

The Dudjom Tersar Lineage of Chatral Rinpoche

Samantabhadra (Dharmakaya realm)

↓

Vajrasattva (Sambhogakaya realm)

↓

Garab Dorje (Nirmanakaya realm)

↓

Manjushrimitra

↓

Sri Singha

↓

Guru Padmasambhava

↓

Khandro Yeshe Tsogyal

↓

Terchen Dudjom Lingpa
(1835–1904)

↓　　　　　　↘

Gyurme Ngedon Wangpo　　Dorje Dradül
↓　　　　　　(1891–1959)

Dudjom Rinpoche
(1904–1987)　　　　↙

↓

Chatral Sangye Dorje Rinpoche
(1913 to present)

Appendix II

The Longchen Nyingthig Lineage of Chatral Rinpoche

Samantabhadra (Dharmakaya realm)

↓

Vajrasattva (Sambhogakaya realm)

↓

Garab Dorje (Nirmanakaya realm)

↓

Manjushrimitra

↓

Sri Singha

↓

Yeshe Do

↓

Vimalamitra

↓

Guru Padmasambhava

↓

Longchen Rabjam

(1308–1363)

↓

Rigzin Jigme Lingpa

(1729–1798)

↓

Jigme Gyalwai Nyugu

(1765–1843)

↓

Patrul Rinpoche

(1808–1887)

↓

Lungtok Tenpai Nyima

(1829–1901)

↓

Khenpo Ngawang Palzang

(1879–1941)

↓

Chatral Sangye Dorje Rinpoche

(1913 to present)

Appendix III

The Sera Khandro Lineage of Chatral Rinpoche

Tersay Drimed Özer
(1881-1924)

↙   ↘

Khandro Dewai Dorje   Chödak Tsultrim Dorje
(1899–1952)

↘   ↙

Chatral Sangye Dorje Rinpoche
(1913 to present)

Appendix IV

"The Seven-Line Prayer to Guru Rinpoche"

HÜNG ORGYEN YÜL GI NÜB CHANG TSAM
HUNG On the northwest border of the country of Uddiyana,

PEMA GESAR DÖNG PO LA
On the pistil of a lotus,

YA TSEN CHÖG GI NGÖ DRÜB NYE
You have attained the most marvelous, supreme accomplishments.

PEMA JÜNG NAY SHAY SU DRA
You are renowned as the Lotus Born

KHOR DÜ KHANDRO MANGPO KOR
Surrounded by your retinue of many dakinis.

KHAY KI JE SÜ DÄG DRÜB GI
Following you in my practice,

CHIN GI LOB CHIR SHÉ SU SOL
I pray you will come to confer your blessings.

GURU PEMA SIDDHI HÜNG
Oh Lotus-Born Guru, please help me to attain your accomplishments.

Notes

Chapter 1

1. Kyabje means "Lord of Refuge" and is a title given to highly revered figures in Tibetan Buddhism.
2. Chatral Rinpoche was born on the tenth day of the fifth month of the Tibetan New Year, which in 1913 was the Water Ox Year. This day generally falls sometime in June. His birthday is on the same day that Guru Padmasambhava took the form of Guru Dorje Drölo, a wrathful manifestation he took in Bhutan in order to subdue the local deities and guardians and convert them into protectors of the hidden terma teachings.
3. Dudjom Rinpoche, *Practice of the Mountain Retreat Expounded Simply and Directly in Its Essential Nakedness.*
4. Terma means "treasure" and refers to the hundreds of teachings hidden by Guru Padmasambhava throughout Tibet to be discovered by "treasure revealers" called tertöns. See Chapter 6 for more details about terma.
5. See Appendix I for the Dudjom Tersar lineage chart.
6. See Appendix III for the Sera Khandro lineage chart.
7. Khenpo Ngawang Palzang, who was popularly referred to as Khenpo Ngakchung, is likened to the central figure of the Longchen Nyingthig Tradition — Longchen Rabjam — in his vast scholarship and high realization (see also note 127). In fact, he had many visions of Longchen Rabjam in which he received empowerments and teachings from him. He performed miracles as a young child, including reversing the flow of a river with a stick fashioned as a ritual dagger to avert a flood. Such remarkable signs caused him to be recognized as Vimalamitra's manifestation. Khenpo Ngakchung became the heart disciple of Lungtok Tenpai Nyima at a young age and received the full Longchen Nyingthig transmissions from him. He studied extensively

107

at Dzogchen Monastery and engaged in several retreats to master the teachings. He also wrote famous texts on trekchöd and tögyal and served as the abbot of Kathok Monastery for many years.

8. Lungtok Tenpai Nyima was also known as Nyoshul Lungtok.

9. Dzogchen (Tib. *rdzogs pa chen po*) means "Great Perfection" and refers to the highest teachings of the Nyingma lineage tradition.

10. The Longchen Nyingthig tradition is the primary lineage for the practice of Dzogchen by the "Ancient Translation School" of Tibetan Buddhism known as Nyingma (see note 27). Longchen Nyingthig means "Heart Essence of the Vast Expanse" (see Appendix II for the Longchen Nyingthig lineage chart).

11. Ngöndro means "preliminary practices." See *The Words of My Perfect Teacher* by Patrul Rinpoche for more details on the Longchen Nyingthig ngöndro.

12. Trekchöd means "cutting through to primordial purity."

13. Tögyal means "crossing over to spontaneous presence."

14. Khyentse Chökyi Lödro was an outstanding master who was an authority on nearly all traditions and holder of nearly all lineages of Tibetan Buddhism. He was a major figure in the *rimay* (Tib. *ris med*) nonsectarian ecumenical movement in Tibet.

15. Yeshe Thaye and Pema Lhadren, "The Life Story of the Lord of Refuge," *Light of Lotus*, Issue 3, June 2000, 11.

16. Ibid., 24.

17. Carroll Dunham and Ian Baker, *Tibet: Reflections from the Wheel of Life*. See http://www.kalachakra.org/articles/pilgrims.shtml.

18. Dudjom Rinpoche, op. cit.

19. Thaye and Lhadren, "The Life Story of the Lord of Refuge," 25.

20. Ibid.

21. It is part of one's bodhisattva vow to come back to help beings in as many future lives as it takes to free them all from suffering. Known as *tulkus* or "emanation bodies," these great beings — including the Dalai Lama — are referred to by the surname "Rinpoche" (pronounced *rin-po-ché*) or "precious one."

22. A dakini is a female celestial being who, among other things, assists Guru Padmasambhava with the discovery and dissemination of terma teachings.

23. Thaye and Lhadren, "The Life Story of the Lord of Refuge," 12.

24. The name of the Chogyur Lingpa terma being transmitted.

25. Erik Pema Kunsang and Marcia Binder Schmidt, *Blazing Splendor: The Memoirs of Tulku Urgyen Rinpoche*, 304–305.

26. Guru Padmasambhava is known as the "Second Buddha," as Shakyamuni Buddha told his disciples that he would manifest again in eight years time and teach tantra — the advanced practices of Buddhism through which one can attain enlightenment in just one lifetime. Guru Padmasambhava is said to have emerged from a lotus in the form of an eight-year-old boy in Uddiyana (believed to be in the present-day Swat Valley), as predicted. He had eight major manifestations in which he studied and practiced tantra. He was invited by King Trisong Deutsen (790–844) to pacify the forces preventing the introduction of Buddhism in Tibet, so he came to Tibet and subdued many demons and wrathful spirits who became protectors of Buddhism. With the help of the great master Khenpo Shantarakshita, he established Samye Monastery as the country's first Buddhist monastery, thus successfully introducing Buddhism to Tibet.

27. The Nyingma School is the oldest of the four main schools of Tibetan Buddhism; the other three are the Sakya, Kagyu, and Geluk schools. Among the great luminaries in the Nyingma tradition are Kyabje Dilgo Khyentse Rinpoche, Kyabje Nyoshul Khen Rinpoche, and Kyabje Dudjom Rinpoche.

28. Yönru Chimey Dorje predicted before Chatral Rinpoche was born, "The supreme manifestation of Guru Padmasambhava's mind/ The child blessed by Vimalamitra/Born in the Ox Year by the name of Vajra/Will spread the lineage of practice" (from Thaye and Lhadren, "The Life Story of the Lord of Refuge," 10). Vimalamitra was one of the great figures in the Nyingma School during Guru Padmasambhava's time and Khenpo Ngawang Palzang is considered to be his emanation.

29. On March 10, 1959, thousands of Tibetans in Lhasa — concerned that the Dalai Lama's safety was in jeopardy — staged a massive uprising that lasted three days and left scores dead. The Chinese brutally suppressed the uprising and afterwards the Dalai Lama fled over the Himalayas into India. Since then, hundreds of thousands of

Tibetans have gone into exile in Nepal, Bhutan, India, Europe, and the United States.

30. Guru Padmasambhava had prophesied, "When the iron bird flies and horses run on wheels, the Tibetan people will be scattered across the face of the earth and the Dharma will come to the land of the red faces."

31. Thaye and Lhadren, "The Life Story of the Lord of Refuge," 26.

32. From an interview with Chatral Rinpoche in 2000, published in *Nonviolence in Tibetan Culture*, a Fieldwork Project for the University of Wisconsin-Madison College Year in Nepal program. The first section, "Finding the Dharma in a Flesh-Based Diet," is available at http://online.sfsu.edu/~rone/Buddhism/BuddhismAnimalsVegetarian/VegMeatTibet.htm.

33. *Sangyüm* means "consort" or "wife." Unlike monks, it is not uncommon for yogis to take consorts in the later stages of their lives. Other great yogis such as Dilgo Khyentse Rinpoche and Nyoshul Khen Rinpoche also had consorts later in their lives.

34. Dharmakaya means "Dharma Body" and refers to the primordial state of perfect awareness.

35. *The Asian Journal of Thomas Merton.* New York: New Directions Books, 1968, 143–144.

36. A stupa is a Buddhist monument with a square base, a lotus flower-shaped middle, and a conical top, filled with sacred Buddhist texts and relics. Buddhists make a pilgrimage to a stupa by circumambulating it clockwise and saying prayers. The Boudhanath Stupa in the Kathmandu Valley, perhaps the largest and most famous stupa in the world, is the focal point for the Tibetan community in Nepal.

37. Thaye and Lhadren, "The Life Story of the Lord of Refuge," 39.

38. There are many stories of Chatral Rinpoche testing Western students who asked for teachings to check if the level of their devotion was sufficient. One man was told that if he picked up a poisonous snake that was lying in the grass, he could be Rinpoche's disciple. Reportedly, the man picked up the snake and was then allowed to study at one of Rinpoche's centers. Such harsh tests are not uncommon, in order to determine if the level of devotion to the master is

sufficient for the disciple to benefit from the teachings. Milarepa's master Marpa put him through similarly stringent tests.

39. Chökyi Nyima Rinpoche is a lama of both the Kagyu and Nyingma Schools of Tibetan Buddhism. He has many Western disciples who study at his center in Boudha, Nepal, popularly known as "The White Gompa."

40. This refers to realization of the four kayas (Nirmanakaya, Sambhogakaya, Dharmakaya, and Svabhavikakaya) without reference point of the three times (past, present, and future).

41. The state of primordial awareness beyond conceptual thought.

42. See http://gomde.dk/pages/biography/cnyima/mayum1.htm.

43. See Appendix IV for "The Seven-Line Prayer to Guru Padmasambhava."

44. See http://www.vajrayana.org/7line.html.

45. See http://pages.cthome.net/tibetanbuddhism/thangka_qualifications.htm.

46. Sogyal Rinpoche, *The Tibetan Book of Living and Dying*. San Francisco: HarperCollins, 1994, 269–270.

47. From *The Thirty-seven Practices of a Bodhisattva*, see http://buddhism.kalachakranet.org/resources/37_practices_Bodhisattva.html.

48. Thaye and Lhadren, "The Life Story of the Lord of Refuge," 38.

49. A high level of meditative absorption in which the nondual nature of mind is experienced.

50. Khenpo Tendzin Özer, "Seed of Faith: A Biography of the Lord of Refuge, Chatral Sangye Dorje," translated by Erik Pema Kunsang. In this excerpt, the word "JVALA" has been changed to "with the radiant syllable"; the words "letter YAM" have been changed to "syllable YAM"; the words "element of KHAM" have been changed to "elemental syllable KHAM".

51. Thaye and Lhadren, "The Life Story of the Lord of Refuge," 10.

Chapter 2

52. Tsetan Chonjore assisted in the translation of this interview, which was recorded at Yangleshöd in 2000.

53. The great master Virupa was drinking one evening at a tavern and

the bartender told him that he could drink as much as he wanted for free until sundown. As he did not have any money on him, he stuck his *purba* (ritual dagger) into the ground at the confluence of the shadow and the sunlight, causing both to stay where they were and preventing the sun from setting.

54. Thaye and Lhadren, "The Life Story of the Lord of Refuge," 34.

55. *Phowa* is the practice of transferring one's consciousness through the central channel out through the top of the head, known as the "Brahma's door." The consciousness is then envisioned as entering the heart of Buddha Amitabha. In this way, one can better control the nature of one's next incarnation at the moment of death.

56. Thaye and Lhadren, "The Life Story of the Lord of Refuge," 34.

57. *Lankavatara Sutra* (Tib. *lang kar gshegs pa'i mdo*).

58. In Buddhist cosmology, there are six realms of samsaric existence, all marked by their own types of suffering. The god realm is marked by laziness and subsequent lack of accumulated merit, which leads to the dread of descending into lower realms at the end of their long and luxurious lives. The jealous gods (*asuras*) have a lush life, but are always fighting out of envy. The human realm is marked by the suffering of birth, old age, sickness, and death; the suffering experienced when things change; the suffering that compounds previous suffering; and the suffering resultant from prior negative action. The animal realm is marked by ignorance; animals cannot speak to other species and so are easily exploited by humans and are often in helpless or fearful situations. Hungry ghosts (*pretas*) have insatiable desire and attachment, and are described as having tiny mouths and huge bellies, causing them to be perpetually hungry and thirsty. The sixth realm represents anger and hatred and includes eight types of hot hells, eight types of cold hells, and two additional types of hells. Chatral Rinpoche is referring to two types of hot hells — the boiling and burning hells.

59. A shravaka is a type of highly accomplished Buddhist meditation practitioner according to the Theravayana tradition.

60. *Lankavatara Sutra* (Tib. *Lang kar gShegs pa'i mDo*).

61. Parinirvana refers to the Buddha's physical passing from the human realm into the state of perfect Enlightenment.

62. The four root principles are refraining from the following: sexual misconduct, killing, stealing, and lying.

63. The seven classes of vinaya vows are monk's vows, nun's vows, novice monk's vows, novice nun's vows, intermediate nun's vows, male lay practitioner's vows, and female lay practitioner's vows.

64. An advanced yogi such as Tilopa can liberate animals like fish by consuming their dead body parts. Another advanced yogic practice is to eat that which is normally taboo, viewing it as pure nectar in its essence.

65. *Chöd* means "cut" and is a practice for destroying ego-clinging by offering your body, cut into pieces and converted into pure nectar, as sustenance for the enlightened ones, the hungry ghosts, demons, and other sentient beings. It is traditionally practiced at charnel grounds and cemeteries.

66. The lama Arya Katayana once visited a family on his begging rounds in which he could see through his clairvoyance that the father of the husband living in the house — who had died a few years earlier — had been reborn as a fish the family was now having for dinner. The dog of the house had been the husband's mother and their enemy had been reborn as their son. The husband's stepmother was also at the table. Arya Katayana was quoted as saying, "He eats his father's flesh; he kicks his mother away. He dandles on his lap the enemy that he killed. The wife is gnawing at her husband's bones. I laugh to see what happens in samsara's show!" From Patrul Rinpoche, *Words of My Perfect Teacher*, 50.

67. Tsele Natsok Rangdrol (*rTse le sNga tshogs Rang grol*, 1608–?).

68. "Triple refuge" means taking refuge in the Buddha, Dharma (the Buddha's teachings), and Sangha (the spiritual community).

Chapter 3

69. A ushnisha is a cranial protuberance that represents the enlightened mind of a Buddha.

70. Yidam means "deity" and refers here to the deity of compassion, Avalokiteshvara.

71. Buddha Amitayus is the buddha of long life (conventionally) and

infinite life (ultimately) who dwells in the pure realm of Akanishta with the Buddha Amitabha.

72. Siddhas are spiritually perfected practitioners who have attained the highest accomplishments.

73. This refers to Lord Yama, who represents the cause and effect principle that determines the nature of one's next incarnation.

74. MAMA KOLING SAMANTA is a closing mantra in Sanskrit recited for the liberation of all beings.

Chapter 4

75. The five inexpiable sins are killing one's mother, killing one's father, killing an Arhat, causing schism in the Sangha, and drawing blood from a Buddha with evil intent.

76. One who will not turn back on the path to Buddhahood.

77. The Dedication of Merit prayer composed by Chatral Rinpoche for "A Brief Summary of the Benefits of Building, Circumnambuting, Prostrating to, and Making Aspirations Prayers at a Stupa" is given at the end of the book.

Chapter 5

78. The "Mind-mandate Transmission" serves as a key to unlock the encoded terma when the terton discovers it.

79. Thondup, Tulku, *Hidden Teachings of Tibet: An Explanation of the Terma Tradition of the Nyingma School of Buddhism.* London: Wisdom Publications, 1986, 103.

80. Dudjom Rinpoche explains why this so is in his famous *Richo* text: "It is because the Dzogpachenpo is so very profound that there will be obstacles, just as making a great profit entails a great risk. The reason for this is that all the negative karma accumulated in the past is churned up by the potency of the oral instructions, and as a sign of this, it arises externally as obstacles and apparitions created by Mara." From Dudjom Rinpoche, *Richo*, Paris: Rigpa, 1987, 15. When mental projections appear in the form of spirits and so forth, the practitioner needs to have reached the

level of being able to recognize them instantly as manifestations of the mind.

81. Buddha Shakyamuni

82. Guru Padmasambhava

83. Avalokiteshvara, Manjushri, and Vajrapani are the deity of compassion, the deity of wisdom, and the wrathful deity known as "The Lord of Secrets" who represents the power and strength of all the buddhas, respectively. They are the three most prominent figures among what are known as the "Eight Great Bodhisattvas" and abide in the Sambhogakaya realm.

84. The earth, the heavens, and the emanated worlds.

85. The Three Roots are the Guru, Deity, and Dakini.

Chapter 6

86. Ian Baker, *The Heart of the World: A Journey to the Last Secret Place*, 2004, 25–26.

87. Rushen is a Dzogchen preliminary practice of distinguishing the dualistic mind from nondual awareness, in order to weaken the notion of an independent self.

88. Baker, *The Heart of the World*, 452. "Nyen sa chöd" has been replaced with "chöd" by the editor.

89. A tambura is an unfretted lute of India, used as a drone.

90. Amitayus belongs to the padma (lotus) family of the buddhas.

91. This refers to White Tara, the female buddha invoked in long-life practices.

92. The third deity of long life is Namgyalma (Ushnivijaya in Sanskrit), who is white in color with three faces and eight arms.

93. Haleshi is the Nepali name for Maratika.

94. Shiva is the Hindu god of creation and destruction and Umadevi is his female counterpart. Maratika is famous for its sacred Shiva linga and formerly had a 120-ft.-high statue of Shiva at the site.

95. Chakrasamvara is a blue-black, four-faced, twelve-armed deity, one of the main Herukas, often depicted with his consort.

96. Akanishta is considered the very highest plane of existence.

97. One of the manifestations of Guru Padmasambhava.

98. During an empowerment, the initiate "enters the mandala" of the deity in question to receive the blessings of that deity. Guru Padmasambhava and Princess Mandarava entered the mandala of Amitayus in a very real way, thus receiving the empowerment of immortality directly.

99. The rakshas are cannibal demons who dwell on an island imperceptible to humans, to which Guru Padmasambhava went when he left Tibet.

100. Chatral Rinpoche himself is considered a mind emanation of Guru Padmasambhava.

101. The Jokhang is the most famous temple in Lhasa and is located near the Potala Palace.

102. Milk, butter, and yogurt.

103. "EMA" is the abbreviated form of "EH MA HO," which means "How marvelous!"

Chapter 7

104. The fivefold certainties are: the certain place, which is the Densely Arrayed (Tib. *'og min stug po bkod*); the certain form, which is adorned with the marks and signs; the certain teaching, which is exclusively the Mahayana; the certain retinue, which is only bodhisattvas of the ten bhumis; and the certain time, which is unceasing or for as long as Samsara lasts.

105. I believe this relates to the experience of the bardo. For an ordinary being, the fivefold vision relate to the nature of their rebirth (fire for hell-bound beings, forests for animal-bound beings, heavenly abodes for god-realm-bound beings, and so on). For enlightened beings, these five visions are not fearful, but are opportunities to benefit beings out of their compassion.

106. Earth.

107. Manjushri, Avalokiteshvara, and Vajrapani.

108. Renunciation, study, and work.

109. These are the degeneration of human longevity, the degeneration of the environment, the degeneration of the views of beings, the degeneration of the faculties of beings, and the degeneration of attitudes in having increased negativity.

110. The three outer tantras and the three inner tantras of Mahayoga, Anuyoga, and Atiyoga (Dzogchen).
111. Above, on, and below earth.

Chapter 8

112. The following lines have been omitted: "In this regard if you ask who made this request, it was made to those of us who are very old by the sponsor Tarthang Tulku Rinpoche, who initiated this event and took responsibility for the first gathering with great kindness. Later on, the responsibility of organizing the event was rotated among various teachers who displayed great kindness in doing so. I am very grateful to them."
113. The following lines have been omitted: "In any case, just as we have elected Kyabje Drubwang Pema Norbu Rinpoche as the leader of the Nyingma Tradition this year; he too — with a vast altruistic motivation and the blessings and prayers of his predecessor as well as the activities of the oceanlike protectors of the Dharma — is accomplishing vast benefits for the Dharma and sentient beings. For us, having left behind our homeland, we had to seek refuge in the noble lands of India, Nepal, Sikkim, and Bhutan. Many of us had a hard time even just finding enough food to eat. Even if we had some opinions on the matter, we had no means to express them."
114. The sixfold greatness of the Early Translation School includes the sponsors who invited the translators, the place of translation, the translators themselves, the scholars who assisted in the translation, the offering gifts made during the translation process, and the translated teachings.
115. This is most likely a reference to the multiplicity of recognized tulkus of the late, great Dudjom Rinpoche. Chatral Rinpoche is discouraging Nyingmapas from making an issue out of this to avoid the devastating consequences of the controversy in which the situation of having two recognized tulkus of the Karmapa, the leader of the Kagyu School, has created an ugly conflict.
116. Bodhicitta is the motivation to attain enlightenment in order to help all others do the same.

117. The bardo is the intermediary stage between physical death and one's next rebirth.

118. See note 109.

119. *'Jam dPal mTshan brJod*

120. *sMon Lam Chen po bZang po sPyod pa*

121. *Thub Chog Byin rLabs gTer mDzod* is a sadhana focused on Shakyamuni Buddha.

122. This refers to *'Khor gSum Yongs Dag*, a practice that is free from the concepts of a subject, an object, and an action.

123. Mara is the equivalent of "devil" and is the Buddhist embodiment of evil.

124. Guru Padmasambhava famously said that even though his view was higher than the sky, his conduct with regard to cause and effect was finer than barley flour.

125. "Emanation bodies" — high lamas who have decided to reincarnate again as teachers in order to help all beings.

126. Abbots.

127. Longchen Rabjam, also known as Longchenpa, was the preeminent scholar of the Dzogchen tradition. He systematized the Nyingma doctrine in his great work, *Seven Treasures*, and was a holder of all the major Dzgochen lineage teachings.

128. If you do the prayers improperly, you carry the burdens of those deceased people with you when you yourself die.

129. A puja is a worship service where offerings such as food are made to the deities, buddhas, and bodhisattvas and subsequently to all beings. After the service, the participants eat much of the offered food as a source of blessings.

130. Samaya is the karmic connection between the student and disciple and includes a set of promises made to the teacher, such as following the practices well, viewing the teacher with a pure mind, and so forth.

131. The following lines have been omitted: "This festival isn't for many years or months. Keeping in mind that it is only for ten days, we should not make any mistakes until it ends."

132. Discipline, concentration, and wisdom.

133. The Statements of the Tripitaka are the three collections of the

Buddha's teachings: Vinaya, Sutra, and Abhidharma. The Vinaya includes teachings about monastic discipline and ethics. The Sutras are the Buddha's concise teachings to his disciples. The Abhidharma is the foundation for Buddhist psychology, logic, and cosmology.

134. This refers to *zhing sa*, an atmosphere where the seed of Buddhahood can grow and flourish.

135. In a monastic hall, there are several rows where monks sit. Being the head of a sitting row involves some prestige.

136. A chakra is an eight-spoked wheel, symbolic of the Dharma.

137. The past, present, future, and time beyond time.

138. Earth, water, fire, and wind.

Chapter 9

139. "Homage to the Spiritual Master."

140. Pema Ledrel Tsal is one of the names Chatral Rinpoche uses to refer to his teacher Khenpo Ngawang Palzang.

141. Virtuous actions should be adopted; negative actions should be abandoned.

142. The five poisons are anger, desire, ignorance, pride, and envy.

Long-Life Prayers

143. Guru Padmasambhava.

144. The two benefits are the benefit of attaining liberation oneself and the benefit of helping all others attain liberation.

145. Khenpo Tendzin Özer, "Seed of Faith," 6. In this prayer, "Kharchu Sa" has been changed to "Guru Padmasambhava's mind" and "triple worlds" has been changed to "three worlds" by the editor.

146. Samantabhadra is the Buddha of the Dharmakaya realm and represents the primordial state of perfect awareness.

147. Supreme bodhicitta is the recognition of the Buddha nature in all sentient beings and subsequently their primordial purity, and occurs when one realizes the inseparability of emptiness and compassion, at which point limitless compassion emanates spontaneously from this awareness.

148. At the end of any teaching or practice, it is obligatory to dedicate the merit of that activity to the benefit of all beings in their quest for enlightenment. Having read through this book and contemplated the teachings of the great master Chatral Rinpoche, all its readers have created merit and, by saying this prayer, all the benefits of this merit will be secured.

Sources

The Asian Journal of Thomas Merton. Edited by Naomi Burton, Patrick Hart, and James Laughlin. New York: New Directions Publications, 1968.

Blazing Splendor: The Memoirs of Tulku Urgyen Rinpoche. Erik Pema Kunsang and Marcia Binder Schmidt. Kathmandu: Rangjung Yeshe Publications, 2005.

The Heart of the World. Ian Baker. New York: Penguin Press, 2004.

Hidden Teachings of Tibet: An Explanation of the Terma Tradition of the Nyingma School of Buddhism. Tulku Thondup Rinpoche. Edited by Harold Talbott. London: Wisdom Publications, 1986.

The Lankavatara Sutra: A Mahayana Text. Translated by D.T. Suzuki. New Delhi: Munshiram Manoharlal Publishers, 1999.

Light of Lotus. Edited by Dr. David Kin-keung Chan. Hong Kong: Dudjom Buddhist Association, Issue 3, June 2000.

Mayüm's Life. Chökyi Nyima Rinpoche. Translated by Erik Pema Kunsang. See http://gomde.dk/pages/biography/cnyima/mayum1.htm.

The Tibetan Book of Living and Dying. Sogyal Rinpoche. San Francisco: HarperCollins, 1995.

Practice of the Mountain Retreat Expounded Simply and Directly in Its Essential Nakedness. Dudjom Rinpoche. Translated by Matthieu Ricard. Darjeeling, India: OKC Monastery, 1976.

Seed of Faith: A Biography of the Lord of Refuge, Chatral Sangye Dorje. Khenpo Tendzin Özer. Translated by Erik Pema Kunsang. 2003 (unpublished).

The Thirty-seven Practices of a Bodhisattva. Thogmed Zangpo. See http://buddhism.kalachakranet.org/resources.

The Words of My Perfect Teacher. Patrul Rinpoche. Translated by Padmakara Translation Group. San Fransisco: HarperCollins Publishers, 1994.

Index

Shambhala Publications
2129 13th Street
US-CO, 80302
US
https://www.shambhala.com
617-424-0030

The authorized representative in the EU for product safety and compliance is

Eucomply OÜ
Pärnu mnt 139b-14
CZ, 11317
EE
https://www.eucompliancepartner.com
hello@eucompliancepartner.com
372 536 865 02

ISBN: 9781559392716
Release ID: 150698198

Printed in the United States
by Baker & Taylor Publisher Services